Doing enterprise architecture

Process and practice in the real enterprise

Tom Graves

Tetradian Consulting

Published by
Tetradian Books
Unit 215, Communications House
9 St Johns Street, Colchester, Essex CO2 7NN
England

http://www.tetradianbooks.com

First published April 2009
ISBN 978-1-906681-18-0 (paperback)
ISBN 978-1-906681-19-7 (e-book)

Contents

Acknowledgements

Amongst others, the following people kindly provided comments and feedback on the early drafts of this book: Michael Ater (Promis, CH), Daljit Banger (White Knight Consulting, GB), Stuart Curley (Royal Mail, GB), Charles Edwards (ProcessWave, GB), Geoff Elliott (Ado Consulting, GB), Nigel Green (CapGemini, GB), Bas van Gils (Deventer, NL), Ziggy Jaworowski (NSW DoCS, Aus), Alexander Lörke (Royal Mail, GB), Graham McLeod (Promis, SA), Bob MacDonald (Telstra, Aus), Helen Mills (Australia Post, Aus), Jos van Oosten (Q-Tips, NL), Kim Parker (Australia Post, Aus), Liz Poraj-Wilczynska (Brockhampton, GB), Erik Proper (CapGemini, NL), Marlies van Steenbergen (Sogeti, NL), Kevin Smith (Pragmatic EA, GB), Peter Tseglakof (Australia Post, Aus), Jaco Vermeulen (Chaos Based, GB).

Please note that, to preserve commercial and personal confidentiality, the stories and examples in this book have been adapted, combined and in part fictionalised from experiences in a variety of contexts, and do not and are not intended to represent any specific individual or organisation.

INTRODUCTION

Doing enterprise architecture

Enterprise architecture is a relatively new discipline, though one that is rapidly becoming more important in business, especially in large multi-partner enterprises. But what do enterprise architects actually *do*? And what kind of business value can be assigned to the results of that work? To put it in the baldest business terms, what's the return on investment?

Enterprise architects manage a body of knowledge about enterprise structure and purpose. There are a fair few books available now about the principles and even some of the overall practices. (You'll find a selection of books and other key references on this listed in the *Resources* section at the end of this chapter.) But in most cases, that's about as far as they go. What this book does instead is focus on what is done in practice, in what order, and *why* it is done – the real business concerns that need to be addressed at each level of architecture maturity.

At present, enterprise architecture is often described solely as an aspect of IT, responsible for improving 'business/IT alignment'. But in practice, it can, and should, cover a much broader scope than just IT. Although it will often start out from there, it should eventually encompass the architecture of the entire enterprise. So the examples shown here are drawn not only from the usual information-centric industries such as finance, banking, insurance and the like, but also other industries in which IT is merely one of many different 'enablers' – such as in telecoms, logistics, utilities, manufacturing, government and much else besides.

Enterprise-architecture is a strategic skill that can be of real value to *every* enterprise, regardless of its size, its type, its industry or context. The same principles apply as much to a theatre, an engineering works, a retail floor, a chemical plant or a bank: it really doesn't matter. And in some aspects of enterprise architecture there may be no IT at all: as one commentator put it, an enterprise has an architecture even if it doesn't have electricity.

Whatever your enterprise, this book will show you what to do, when and how and why, to make it all work in practice.

Who should read this book?

This book is intended for enterprise architects, strategists and any others tasked with understanding the enterprise as a whole; and for programme and portfolio managers and others who guide the changes to business practice that arise from that work.

Enterprise-architecture provides a 'big-picture' overview that outlines the business context for other architecture disciplines: so this book would also be useful for business architects, process architects, security architects, solution architects, software architects and the like.

And executives, service-managers, process-managers and many others may find this book valuable as a guide to what enterprise architects do, and why they do what they do, in support of the overall enterprise.

What's in this book?

There are three main parts to this book. The first deals with what's involved in setting up the architecture capability, and getting down to work - see *Preparing for architecture*, p.5. Next, we explore the typical kinds of work, and the business concerns they each address, at each stage of enterprise-architecture maturity - see *A matter of maturity*, p.29. Finally, we'll explore what you'd do to keep on enhancing the depth and richness and value of the architecture capability and its artefacts - see *What next?*, p.165.

Each section includes lists of questions to guide the work. These lists are fairly comprehensive, but obviously cannot cover everything - given the vast range of possible circumstances in which they may be used - and in some cases the questions themselves must necessarily be somewhat generic. So whilst you should find all the essentials here, do expect to do some translation and adaptation to suit your own specific context.

What's *not* in this book? In essence, anything that is context-specific, or is easily available elsewhere. For example, you'll need a suitable architecture-development method: for that, you might turn to the current *de facto* standard, TOGAF™ Version 9 - all 780 pages of it, for which obviously there's no point in repeating here.

> Since TOGAF is designed only for enterprise IT-architecture, you may want to supplement it with *Bridging the Silos: enterprise architecture for IT-architects*, another book in this series, which shows how to adapt TOGAF to the real whole-of-enterprise scope.

You'll need a suitable reference-framework, or set of frameworks - though these should be chosen from examples tailored to your specific industry, such as eTOM for telecoms, SCOR for logistics or FEAF PRM for government. And you'll need some kind of formal governance-framework, to guide architecture development and its relationship with change-management: but again, this is described in part in the TOGAF specification, and will need to be linked to whatever techniques you already use to govern enterprise change. The same applies to metrics, to detailed definitions of skillsets, and so on: the extra information you'll need there will depend on your context, but you should be able to find that easily enough from your industry's existing sources.

This book deals with the one specific practical concern: what do you *do* when doing enterprise architecture? Our aim has been to keep this book to a practical size that you can keep beside you as you work. So to that end, there are plenty of cross-references in the *Resources* sections at the end of each chapter: use them to fill in any gaps and keep you on track for your own business context.

Resources

The Tetradian Enterprise Architecture Series

- 🕮 Tom Graves, *Real Enterprise Architecture: beyond IT to the whole enterprise* (Tetradian, 2008) - describes a high-level framework and method for whole-of-enterprise architecture
- 🕮 Tom Graves, *Bridging the Silos: enterprise architecture for IT-architects* (Tetradian, 2008) - describes how to adapt and extend IT-architecture *de facto* standards such as Zachman, TOGAF, FEAF, ITIL and PRINCE2 for use at a whole-of-enterprise scope
- 🕮 Tom Graves, *SEMPER and SCORE: enhancing enterprise effectiveness* (Tetradian, 2008) - describes a suite of tools and techniques to enhance enterprise effectiveness, such as the SCORE extension to SWOT strategy-assessment, and the SEMPER diagnostic and metric for enterprise effectiveness
- 🕮 Tom Graves, *Power and Response-ability: the human side of systems* (Tetradian, 2008) - describes the business implications of the dichotomy that whilst the physics definition of 'power' is 'the ability to do work', most social definitions are closer to the ability to avoid it

- Tom Graves, *The Service Oriented Enterprise: enterprise architecture and viable systems* (Tetradian, 2009) – describes how to extend the principle of service-oriented architecture to the design and structure of the entire enterprise

Other resources

- The Open Group, *TOGAF™ Version 9* (Van Haren, 2009)
- Online version of TOGAF 9: see www.opengroup.org/architecture/togaf9-doc/arch/
- FEAF (US Federal Enterprise Architecture Framework): see www.gao.gov/special.pubs/eaguide.pdf [PDF]
- Zachman framework: see www.zifa.com
- ITIL (Information Technology Infrastructure Library): see www.itil.org.uk and www.itil-officialsite.com

PREPARING FOR ARCHITECTURE

What *is* 'enterprise architecture'? It seems traditional to start off a book of this kind with a set of definitions, but here we'd perhaps be better served by a more discursive exploration, because it's surprisingly hard to find anything that's definite and definitive about any aspect of this discipline...

First, perhaps, the 'architecture' part. Definitions from the software industry, from the 1960s onward, tend to emphasise the need for *structure*, a consistent description and consistent set of relationships. Elsewhere, especially from business-architecture, there's more of an emphasis on business *purpose*, on devolving outward from strategy. Somewhere between the two, these need to meld into a mutual balance, about where structure meets with purpose, and purpose is expressed in structure. Hence that earlier description:

Enterprise architects manage a body of knowledge about enterprise structure and purpose.

'Enterprise' is perhaps harder to describe. The usual definition is that it's some kind of group who "coordinate their functions and share information in support of a common mission or set of related missions". The catch is that 'enterprise' is *not* the same as 'organisation' - or rather, that a formal organisation such as a company or government department is just one special case of an enterprise.

> Hence perhaps *the* key distinction between business architecture and enterprise architecture: the former would formulate their strategies and suchlike from the organisation's point of view, whilst the latter must also look at least one step above and pay detailed attention to the common enterprise that is shared by all stakeholders.

So unlike business-architects, who maintain focus on the strategic concerns of the company, enterprise architects must be able to work at any level, at any scope. Typically, they will deal more with overview than with detail, though early-maturity enterprise-architecture will often hold a firm emphasis on the finer details of IT-system design.

In essence, though, it's not just about improvements in IT-systems, or in the infamous and often troublesome 'business/IT alignment', but about creating a better understanding of how everything in the enterprise works with everything else – IT, people, machines, strategies, tactics, processes, products, services, *everything*. And it's not just about improved efficiency, but improved *effectiveness* – 'efficient on purpose'.

So where does this all fit, in organisational terms? The short answer is "it all depends", because it'll change with the nature of the enterprise, and usually with the level of architecture maturity. In the early stages it'll often be included within a project, or be a project in its own right; but as maturity develops, it'll need to be set up as a continuing capability, often acting as a bridge between strategy on one side and change-management on the other:

**Strategy specifies requirements for change;
enterprise-architecture identifies capabilities for change;
change-management guides change in the enterprise.**

The common view of enterprise architecture, as espoused in the major standards such as FEAF and TOGAF, is that its role is to define the 'future state' of the structure of the organisation's IT. Amazingly, that assertion manages to be misleading in almost every possible way: it's not just about the organisation, it's not just about the IT, there is no 'the' – there's always '*an* architecture', but never '*the* architecture' – and there is no such thing as a 'future state', because everything is changing dynamically, all the time.

The world is not static: there is no state.

Those standard models then manage to compound the problems by insisting on a 'big-bang' approach to architecture development: we supposedly define 'the future architecture for everything' in one big project, and then it's finished forever. Which simply does not work for a real enterprise architecture: it'll be hopelessly out of date before we're even halfway through the process. It might sort-of work for a small subset of a technology architecture that'll be changed anyway as soon as the next major project comes along, but there's no way to make it work at the scale of a whole enterprise. We *must* think in terms of Agile, of an iterative approach to architecture development, right from the start.

> To be fair, TOGAF's designers do insist that its ADM (Architecture Development Method) could and should be used in an iterative style. Unfortunately, as anyone who's used it in practice will soon discover, TOGAF's predefined scope and structure will fight against this, every

inch of the way. In effect it's a classic Waterfall approach with various bits of Agile vaguely grafted on, but without strict Agile-style governance, and in a way which somehow manages to combine the disadvantages of both without the advantages of either. And in my experience, the attempts to patch the problems in the recent TOGAF 9 upgrade have managed only to make it worse. Oh well.

There are a few enterprise contexts for which a Waterfall approach to architecture would be required: it's all but mandatory in a military environment, for example. But for anything else, the sheer scale of the problems usually means that we *must* use an Agile approach to make it work: and we need to do that Agile properly, too.

But there's a catch here. Without architecture, a framework of context in which to place each iteration, Agile is little more than an undisciplined messing-about: so it seems we'd need an architecture already in place before we can do Agile architecture...

The way out of this dilemma is to cheat: we *invent* an architecture - almost anything that seems appropriate, really - to an act as an initial framework. (More on that when we look at planning and frameworks below - see p.13.) We then refine that framework with each subsequent iteration, steadily filling in more and more detail as we go.

What this is really about is a subtle shift in perspective. The classic Waterfall approach is like a photograph: we don't get the full picture - or, in this context, much if any business value - unless we can see the whole thing in one go. If we cut up a photograph, each small piece contains the full detail of that one area, but gives us no indication of how it fits in with anything else. So until the whole thing - the whole architecture - *is* in place, we're stuck.

By contrast, working with Agile is more like a holograph: we're *always* dealing with the whole picture, right from the start. Everything, however small, is always connected to everything else; and if we cut up a holograph, each small piece always contains a sense of the whole as a whole - the detail will be less, but not the scope. So when we do this right, every project not only delivers its own business value, but also contributes to the business value of everything else - *if* we use the framework holographically.

And we do that by treating every iteration, whatever its scope, in exactly the same way. *Nothing* can be considered 'special and different': so for an Agile architecture, the classic IT-centric style of so-called 'enterprise architecture', with its crass definition of 'business architecture' as "everything not-IT that might impact on IT", would be a guaranteed recipe for failure. To make it work, we have to dump the idea that IT is a special case that somehow *must* be the centre of every enterprise architecture. Instead, we need to view it as just one example amongst all of the business' enablers - a service *to* the business, not the other way round! Which might be a bit uncomfortable for some IT-architects to accept, perhaps: but that's just too bad, bluntly. The business *always* comes first.

Purpose – strategy

All activities in enterprise architecture should begin and end with an explicit business purpose. From the business perspective, architecture is a strategic tool, to guide the implementation of business strategy: so strategy and purpose must always be at its core.

> We need to remember, though, that strategy must always be driven by business need – *not* by IT hype! The fabled 'IT/business alignment' – or, more often, the lack of it – is littered with countless examples of disastrous attempts by consultants, vendors and even IT staff to foist overblown 'solutions' onto a justifiably unwilling business. Business Process Re-engineering (BPR) is perhaps the best known of these, but right now cloud-computing is shaping up nicely as the probable next candidate for the 'Expensive Failure Of The Year Award'…
>
> There's nothing wrong with BPR or cloud-computing as such: they can be very good solutions indeed, *in the right contexts*. Where it all goes wrong is when the 'solution' comes before the strategy, or when it's sold for the wrong reasons – such as the classic IT obsessions with cost-cutting or 'efficiency' for its own sake, without awareness of the broader implications or broader environment. A properly-thought-out, properly-explored strategy must always come before any suggestion of 'solutions': the business and its business-strategy *always* come first.

The real driver for any strategy is enhanced *effectiveness* in the context of continual change. And efficiency is only one of several interweaving strands of effectiveness:

- *efficient* - makes the best use of available resources
- *reliable* - can be relied upon to deliver the required results
- *elegant* - supports the human factors in the context; also 'elegant' in the scientific sense, in that clarity and the like will support structural simplicity and re-use
- *appropriate* - supports and sustains the overall purpose of the enterprise
- *integrated* - everything is linked to and supports the integration of the whole *as* whole

Strategically speaking, it's essential to keep all these strands in balance with each other. If we pay too much attention to any one strand such as efficiency - especially if it's at the expense of the others - we end up with a structure and strategy that might seem to perform well for a while, but is doomed for disaster further down the track. And again, we'll see all too many examples of this in the business press or elsewhere. Whether the strategy is in response to a new opportunity, a change in regulation, a new technology or a new market, the same always applies: we'll need to assess the issue's impact on the *whole* of the enterprise, not just on some selected subsection such as IT. Overall effectiveness *matters*.

> There's more on those effectiveness-themes in two other books in this series, *Real Enterprise Architecture: beyond IT to the whole enterprise* and *SEMPER and SCORE: enhancing enterprise effectiveness* – more details on those in the *Resources* section at the end of the chapter.

The effective purpose of what we do in enterprise architecture will necessarily change at different levels of architecture maturity. For example, there's little point in even *trying* to use architecture to assist in strategy until we have some idea of what business we're in - see *Step 1: Know your business*, p.31 - or made a solid start on cleaning up the chaos that will have arisen naturally from too many mergers and acquisitions, or from too many years without some kind of framework to guide consistency in business systems - see *Step 2: Clean up the mess*, p.65.

More accurately, we don't so much change what we do in architecture as extend it. Each maturity-level builds on those before, but we don't stop doing the work from those previous levels: whatever maturity-level we've reached at, we'll always need to keep track of what business we're in! The same goes for all the subsequent work on system consistency and the like: if we don't stay aware of all the infrastructure changes - new systems coming on-line, old systems reaching their sunset and being retired - we'll risk falling back into the same mess as before.

Strategy on its own is not enough: we also need some consistent means to make it happen, and keep on happening, in the real world of everyday business practice. So for architecture, we need clear metrics, to keep track of what's happening; we need consistent methods, so that we're clear about what needs to happen next; we need a consistent set of frameworks, so we can make sense of what we have and what we're planning to do. But perhaps most all, we need the right skills and structure to make it happen: the right people, and the right kind of governance. Hence it's those issues that we need to turn to next.

People – governance

Strategy describes the 'why' of the business; methods describe the 'how' of what needs to happen; frameworks describe the 'what'; and governance brings us back to 'why' again, by anchoring it in *people* - their choices, their actions and responsibilities.

It's always about people. No matter how technical a problem may seem, ultimately it's always a 'people-problem' - more accurately, it's the skills and commitment and drive of individual people that provide us with the means to solve any given problem.

Where governance comes in is that it's the way by which we manage the people-side of effectiveness - making sure that things happen 'on purpose', in the right order, for the right reasons, and so forth. Formal structures such as ITIL and COBIT and PRINCE2 do this for the IT context in general, for concerns such as service-management and project-management: we now need to do the same for enterprise architecture. Perhaps the key complication is that some of the governance will change quite radically as we move up the maturity scale, but we could summarise the core themes as follows:

- it's not a project - it's a continuing process
- you'll need different skillsets at different maturities
- you'll need senior support - eventually, from the executive and above
- you'll need to identify and engage with a wide range of stakeholders
- it's really about creating an ongoing dialogue about architecture

We'll expand on each of these themes as we explore the different maturity-levels later; for now, though, these are some of the points we'll need to understand before we start.

It's not a project: Enterprise-architecture often starts as a project, or in a project, and ultimately needs to be applied to every project, but it isn't a project in itself. It's a capability whose task is to manage a body of knowledge about structure and purpose - hence, unlike a project, it's not something that we do once and then quietly forget about when it's done. To retain its business value, we need to keep it going, keep it growing, keep putting it to practical use. It's not a project.

You'll need a range of skillsets: At present, enterprise architecture is often described solely as if it's some aspect of IT, and that IT technical skills are the only ones really required. Even if this were true, we would still need to cover the whole scope of 'IT': not just the obvious skills such as data architecture, applications architecture, security architecture, infrastructure architecture, network architecture, service architecture and the like, but building layout, cooling systems, power infrastructures and a whole lot more.

Once we start to move beyond IT to include the rest of the enterprise - especially in industries which are not information-centric, which is true for most - then the required skillsets could be *anything*. At the very least, by the time we reach the second or third maturity-level, we're going to need much more awareness of the business *as* business - which means skillsets in business architecture, organisational architecture, process architecture and so on. So we'll need to plan for that from the start - including all the people-issues of how to cope with those shifts in skillsets, and in the make-up of the enterprise-architecture team.

You'll need senior support: Because enterprise architecture isn't a project, it'll need funding and other resources to keep it going, as a kind of conceptual infrastructure for the enterprise. That can be a whole lot harder than funding a once-off project - but you won't get any real value from enterprise architecture unless you do this.

And as the maturity expands, so does the scope that you'll need to cover. You may well start out as a small 'skunk-works' project tucked away in IT, but by the time you really get going you'll need the authority to touch anywhere in the enterprise, bridge between any of the organisational silos, and ask often awkward questions of just about anyone. To work at that level, you'll need the full weight of the entire executive behind you.

True, you may not need all of that right from the start - though nice to have, of course! - but you'd better plan for it right from the start. Which means you'll need to be able to prove your business value right from the start, too.

You'll need to engage with stakeholders: As the scope of the architecture extends, so too does the range of stakeholders with whom you'll need to engage. Every object, every data-entity, business-rule, business-process and everything else will have a nominal owner - the 'responsible person' - and others who will have a business stake in the use and maintenance of whatever-it-is. And every one of them will want a say in what happens, or at least be kept informed on any possible changes. That's a lot of people - and a lot of resistance to change if you *don't* engage them in the architecture. There's a key point that's worth emphasising here:

People don't resist change: they resist *being* changed.

They'll resist change if they don't see the point in it - in other words, if they suspect it's 'change for change's sake' - and they'll certainly resist it if they think it's solely for someone else's benefit at their own expense. So you need to engage them in the architecture - engage them in *co-creating* enterprise change. If you don't, what you'll get is resistance - lots of it. Your choice...

> Hence the importance of what TOGAF 9 calls a Communication Plan. But even that is nothing like enough: it's not a one-way message to be broadcast after the event. It needs to be a full two-way communication with everyone – a dialogue of equals – that starts from Day One.

It's really about dialogue: Architecture isn't something we can control. It's all too big for that - especially at the scale of an entire enterprise. The only way we'll get it to work is if we share out the load, and preferably amongst everyone in the entire enterprise.

In essence, architecture is just an *idea*: the belief and experience that things work better when they're linked together into a unified whole. Things work better for *everyone* when that happens. But trying to do that by imposing a fixed system of order will only work when the world is static - which the real world isn't. And every small change everywhere impacts on the whole - so we do need to get those changes to work *with* all other parts of the whole. The way we do that is through architecture: more specifically, a continual *dialogue* about architecture.

> It doesn't take a large number of people to guide this dialogue, though. At one of our major clients, a nationwide logistics organisation with some 35000 employees, the core enterprise architecture team consists of just five people – and even they also have other duties outside of architecture itself.
>
> It's much the same with other 'pervasive' themes such as knowledge-management, quality, security, privacy, health and safety: the work is distributed throughout the enterprise, but the core team that 'hold the faith', so to speak, need only be a small handful of specialists.
>
> Or generalists, more accurately – people who link things together across many different domains. In architecture, the specialist domain-architects – data, security, applications, process, service, strategy, infrastructure and so on – are more likely to be attached to project-teams, guiding the detail-concerns of individual change-projects. It's the generalists back at the core who keep the dialogue going, to help hold

everything together. And we don't need many people for that: just a core framework in which people can come and go as needed.

Architecture is also a story, about possibility, and about problems overcome. If we try to force-fit others into someone else's story, it's unlikely they'll be interested in such a predefined part; but if we engage them in *co-creating* the story, they're much more likely to be willing to play. In that sense, engagement *matters*; the story needs to make sense, in a dynamic, personal, visceral way.

Another key complication is that people know more than they can say, and can say more than they can write down. Often the story develops through action and emotion as much as it does through ideas and plans. So the architecture story needs to encompass all those dimensions too - and likewise the framework on which we build and describe and make sense of that story.

Planning – frameworks

In principle, we could describe relationships between everything in the enterprise in terms of a single sentence-structure:

"with «*asset*» do «*function*» at «*location*»
using «*capability*» on «*event*» because «*reason*»"

This comes from a revision of the well-known Zachman framework. It cleans up the taxonomy, and extends the original with an extra row at the top for enterprise core-constants or 'universals', and an extra dimension to clarify scope and implementations:

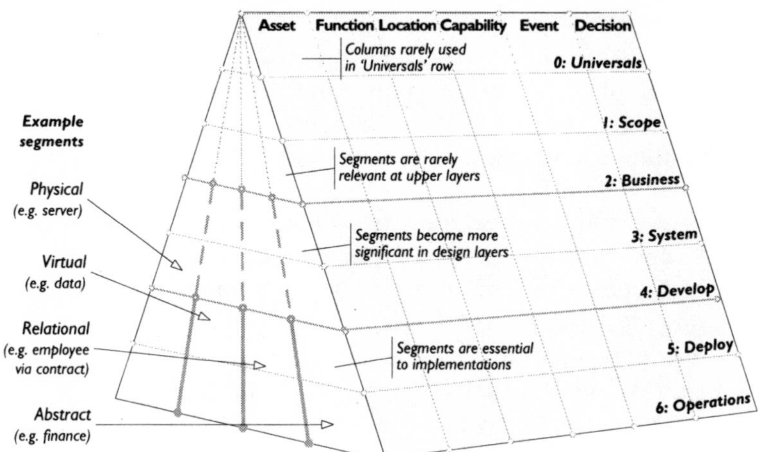

Framework rows, columns and segments

> This is described in more detail in the 'Framework' chapters in another book in this series, *Bridging the Silos: enterprise architecture for IT-architects* – see the *Resources* section below.
>
> See also tetradianbooks.com/ebook/silos_real-ea-frame-ref.pdf for a two-page summary of the framework and its core principles.

For the vertical dimension of the framework, we partition scope in terms of timescale - a set of seven distinct layers or perspectives, from unchanging constants, to items which change moment by moment. Each row adds another concern or attribute:

- *Row 0*: '**Universals**' - in principle, should never change: core constants to which everything should align - identifies the overall region of interest and the key points of connection shared with enterprise partners and other stakeholders; added for compatibility with ISO-9000 etc
- *Row 1*: '**Scope**' (*Zachman*: 'Planner') - adds possibility of change: core entities in each category, in list form, *without* relationships - the key 'items of interest' for the enterprise
- *Row 2*: '**Business**' (*Zachman*: 'Owner') - adds relationships and dependencies between entities: core entities described in summary-form for business-metrics, including relationships between entities both of the same type ('primitives') and of different types ('composites')
- *Row 3*: '**System**' (*Zachman*: 'Designer') - adds attributes to abstract 'logical' entities: entities expanded out into *implementation-independent* designs - includes descriptive attributes
- *Row 4*: '**Develop**' (*Zachman*: 'Builder') - adds details for real-world 'physical' design: entities and attributes expanded out into *implementation-dependent* designs, including additional patterns such as cross-reference tables for 'many-to-many' data-relationships
- *Row 5*: '**Deploy**' (*Zachman*: 'Sub-contractor' or 'Out of Scope') - adds details of intended future deployment: implementation of designs into actual software, actual business-processes, work-instructions, hardware, networks etc
- *Row 6*: '**Operations**' (*Zachman*: implied but not described) - adds details of actual usage: specific instances of entities, processes etc, as created, modified, and acted on in real-time operations

The rows also represent different categories of responsibilities or stakeholders, such as senior management responsible for row-0 universals, or strategists at row-1 and -2, architects and solution-designers at row-3 and -4, and line managers and front-line staff at row-5 and -6. In effect, this is the same layering that we see in the management-hierarchy, and in the nesting of abstract services.

> Strictly speaking, the row-0 'Universals' are more like another dimension or backplane, because *everything* in the enterprise needs to link back to them. Since we already have three dimensions – rows, columns and segments – it's simpler to show it as an extra row at the top, and it's easier for metamodel repositories to implement it that way, too. But it's important to remember, though, that it *is* in effect another framework-dimension in its own right.

Below the core 'Universals', the framework splits horizontally into columns for six distinct categories of primitives, approximating to Zachman's what, how, where, who, when and why:

- *What*: **assets** of any kind – physical objects, data, links to people, morale, finances, etc
- *How*: **functions** – activities or services to create change, described independently from the agent (machine, software, person etc) that carries out that activity
- *Where*: **locations** – in physical space (geography etc), virtual space (IP nodes, http addresses etc), relational space (social networks etc), time and suchlike
- *Who*: **capabilities** clustered as **roles** or 'actors' – may be human, machine, software application, etc, and individual or collective
- *When*: **events** and relationships between those events – may be in time, or physical, virtual, human, business-rule trigger or other event
- *Why*: **decisions**, reasons, constraints and other tests which trigger or validate the condition for the 'reason' and the like, as in strategy, policy, business-requirements, business-rules, regulations etc.

In the lower layers, we also need to split the columns themselves by context into distinct segments or sub-categories. Whilst these could be cut multiple ways, a typical set of segments would be:

- **physical**: tangible objects ('asset'), mechanical processes and functions, physical or temporal locations, physical events; also align to ***rule-based*** skills ('capability') and decisions
- **virtual**: intangible objects such as data ('asset'), software processes and functions, logical locations, data-driven events; also align to ***analytic*** skills ('capability') and decisions

- **relational**: links to people (as indirect 'asset'), manual processes and functions, social/relational locations, human events; also align to ***heuristic*** skills ('capability') and decisions
- **aspirational**: principles and values, brands and belonging, morale and self-belief ('asset'), value-webs and dependencies ('location'), business-rules ('event'); also align with ***principle-based*** skills ('capability') and decisions
- **abstract**: additional uncategorised segments such as financial ('asset', 'function'), energy ('asset'), time (as 'event'-trigger) etc

These are fundamentally different in scope and function:

- *Physical assets* are 'alienable' – if I give it to you, I no longer have it.
- *Virtual assets* are 'non-alienable' – if I give it to you, I also still have it.
- *Relational assets* exist between two entities (usually but not necessarily real people); each is one hundred percent the responsibility of *both* parties – if either party drops it, the relationship ceases to exist – and is actually harder to transfer to someone else than it is to create from scratch.
- *Aspirational assets* have some similarities with relational ones, except that the relationship is more a one-sided 'to' rather than a balanced 'between'.

The enterprise will need to be especially careful how it handles aspirational assets, for example, because they're closely linked to the sense of identity and self, and the passions embedded within them can be extremely destructive if not treated with respect.

> Hence woe betide any company that trashes a much-loved brand, for example, because the intensity of that aspirational commitment can unleash a wave of anger and retribution that resembles the inconsolable rage of grief... It's not 'rational' in any normal sense of the word, but it's definitely real, and does need to be treated as such.
>
> Closer to the opposite extreme, the loss of morale and drive that accompanies 'change-fatigue' has its roots in damage to aspirational assets: specifically, the loss of that sense of belonging, of being part of a known enterprise – an included member of a group who "coordinate their functions and share information in support of a common mission" and so on.
>
> This is crucially important in the architecture of the enterprise, because it's *the* key source of personal drive and commitment to the enterprise. If it's lost, the most we'll get from people is 'presenteeism' – their bodies may be present, but probably not much else. So whilst these can often seem subtle or strange, aspirational assets *matter*.

'Composites' of related entities and entity-types may exist within the same segment in a column, or in different segments of the same column. We can then link these composites across other columns to create other 'incomplete' design-patterns – the kind of structures we usually see in architecture models – or complete the composite across all of the columns for final implementation.

Understanding these asset-categories and the composites created from them helps to describe concerns such as storage and security. For example, a paper form is both a physical asset *and* a virtual asset: we need to manage it as a physical object, with all of the resultant issues around procurement, inventory, pre-use warehousing, modification and use, storage and disposal; yet we *also* need to manage it as a virtual asset, with all those concerns about data-quality, information-quality and so on. And we can describe some of the security-concerns by asset-category as follows:

- *physical security*: protect alienable asset against physical loss
- *virtual security*: protect non-alienable asset against loss via physical means (e.g. theft of laptop, damage to data-server), against inadvertent virtual loss (e.g. deletion, overwrite, out-of-date file-format) and against inadvertent or unauthorised replication
- *relational security*: protect relational asset (e.g. trust) against damage or loss from either end of the relationship
- *aspirational security*: protect aspirational asset against loss at 'near-end' (e.g. arbitrary alteration of brand) and at 'far-end' (e.g. damage to reputation of the brand)

Security for abstract assets such as finance is usually a complex-composite derived from variations of the above.

The various 'pervasives' such as privacy, quality, ethics and the like typically emphasise protection of different combinations of asset-categories, for example:

- *security*: protects physical/virtual assets, also some relational/aspirational assets such as trust
- *privacy*: protects virtual/relational assets
- *health and safety*: protects physical/relational assets
- *ethics and corporate social-responsibility*: protects aspirational/relational assets
- *environment*: protects physical/aspirational assets
- *quality*: generic – protects the asset-categories that apply in the respective business context

All of these may intersect in a sometimes bewildering variety of ways - for example, safety-critical IT-systems may interweave concerns about security, safety, environment and other themes all within a single architectural package.

The balance between incompletion and completion of composites also enables architectural redesign, by anchoring trails of relationship between items or layers, to resolve concerns such as strategic analysis, failure-impact analysis and complex 'pain-points':

Composites are usable when architecturally 'complete'; they are *re*-usable when architecturally '*in*complete'.

The notion of *'bindedness'* - the extent to which a specific composite or primitive should or must be included within a solution - can be used to convert a model into a reference-framework. The obvious example of bindedness is legal compliance, because if we don't comply, we're breaking the law. But it also applies to use of standards of any kind, and many other practical concerns such as whether a particular operating-system or software version or type of milling-machine or whatever should be used in which contexts and for what purposes; and what types of skills and experience would be needed so as to deliver a particular service or decision. Levels of bindedness for any item in a reference-model would typically include:

- *mandatory*: item must be used wherever applicable
- *recommended*: item should be used unless a preferred solution mandates an alternative
- *desirable*: use of the item would aid in consistency
- *suggested*: experience indicates the item may provide a better or more consistent solution than similar alternatives

> Note that these might vary not only according to context, but in many cases will also change over time. Once again, very few items are ever truly static in an enterprise architecture.

Given all this wide variety of information that constitutes the overall framework, you're going to need somewhere to put it, and some systematic means to keep track of it all. At the least, you're going to need:

- *architecture repository*, including models and metamodels, core references, governance documents and other artefacts
- *requirements repository*, documenting requirements, tests for confirmation of those requirements, and relationships between them

- *risk and opportunity registers*, detailing any risks and opportunities identified in architecture, and actions to be taken to address them
- *glossary and thesaurus*, providing standard definitions and cross-references between synonyms, homonyms, heteronyms and the like
- *dispensations register*, recording implementations that have been allowed to not comply with the architecture, the reasons for allowing non-compliance, and how to resolve it in future

Which leads us to another key point, about architecture toolsets. Most people start their architecture with whatever tools come to hand, which typically means standard office applications such as Excel, Visio and PowerPoint. These do work well enough for first experiments, but they don't scale, they don't handle versioning, and they can't manage the myriad of essential cross-connections and cross-references that start to emerge as soon as you begin any serious architecture analysis. So at some stage, and probably sooner rather than later, you'll have to face the facts: you're going to need a proper enterprise-architecture toolset.

> And yes, this will hurt, because all of them are expensive, and all of them have significant or even serious limitations: some of them have user-interfaces that are best described as 'user-hostile', and as yet none of them get close to delivering all of the functionality we need for whole-of-enterprise architecture. But there's no way round it: some kind of purpose-built toolset *is* essential for this type of work.
>
> There's a wide variety of tools out there: some emphasise visual modelling, others more the underlying structures and metamodels. As a consultant and adviser working in many different industries, I prefer the latter, but that's what matches my own needs, whereas your needs may well be different. So I'll avoid making any recommendations here, because the 'right' toolset is the one that works best for you in your own context.
>
> The TOGAF specification provides some useful suggestions – see Chapter 42, 'Tools for Architecture Development', in the TOGAF 9 book or website – and there's an excellent summary of selection-criteria on the Institute for Enterprise Architecture Developments website at www.enterprise-architecture.info/EA_Tools.htm - these should help to ease the pain of picking the right toolset for your needs.

In effect, the framework defines *meaning* within the enterprise and its architecture: and we do need at least some of it in place before we start work. But on its own, the framework does nothing: so the next item we need is a methodology for architecture development.

Practice – methods

Although there are a fair number of formal definitions around for enterprise-architecture, there are surprisingly few that describe methodology - what to *do* in architecture, how to do it, in what sequence, and so on. For most practitioners these days, it almost comes down to a single choice: the Architecture Development method (ADM) that's part of TOGAF, the Open Group's architecture framework.

Which is unfortunate, because whilst it's a good choice for the early stages of enterprise architecture - especially in information-based industries such as insurance and finance - it's essentially focused only on IT, and hence is *not* good for later-maturity architecture, which does need to cover the whole of the enterprise, beyond just its IT. So we need to do some amendments here to make it usable in practice for the whole scope of enterprise architecture, in any industry and at every level of maturity.

> Sadly, this is still true of the latest version, TOGAF 9, which was released only a few weeks ago as I write this. Version 9 is much better-structured than the previous version, '8.1 Enterprise', but it still has the same fixed IT-centric scope, and most of the ancillary information assumes an IT-centred world. It's still useful, though, to read the TOGAF 9 specification, either in the published book or in the online version: see the *Resources* section below for the publication details.
>
> It doesn't matter much to us, anyway: the amendments described here will resolve all those constraints, and will work equally well with either version of TOGAF.

TOGAF's ADM consists of a cycle of eight phases - labelled A to H, and often referred to as 'crop circles'. These are organised in a circle around a central repository for requirements. The first four phases focus on architecture assessment: Architecture Vision for the overall cycle (Phase A); Business Architecture (Phase B) Information Systems Architecture (Phase C), usually split into sub-phases for data- and applications-architecture; and Technology Architecture for IT-infrastructure (Phase D). Phases B to D each have explicit subsidiary steps for 'as-is', 'to-be' and gap-analysis. The second set of four phases deals with defining (Phase E), planning (Phase F) and implementing (Phase G) a 'roadmap' for change, and following through with a final 'lessons-learned' activity (Phase H).

These are all preceded by a 'Preliminary Phase', in which we would set up the architecture capability itself, its governance, and various core documents such as the Architecture Charter and Architecture Principles.

To amend it to work better beyond its inherent over-emphasis on low-level IT, the main changes we need are:

- stronger support for Agile-style development
- allow any scope – not just IT-architecture
- stronger and more explicit integration with governance
- stronger integration with information-repositories

So first, we clear the decks a bit in Phase A. In the original version 8.1, a typical complete architecture cycle would take many months at least. TOGAF 9 allows for more explicit subsidiary iterations within the cycle, but the overall cycle itself still takes as much as a couple of years. What we need instead is something that can still deliver real business value in as little as a couple of hours. To do this, we move much of the content of the existing Phase A back up into the Preliminary Phase, leaving Phase A free to concentrate on the specific details for the current iteration alone.

Next we need to change TOGAF's fixed scope. We can do that very simply, by setting the scope in our amended Phase A, and defined in terms of the respective layers, columns and segments in the framework. We then change the focus of Phase B to D: instead of the previous fixed scope for each phase, with separate 'as-is', 'to-be' and gap-analysis in each, we swap these round such that Phase B covers the 'as-is' for the selected scope, Phase C does the 'to-be', and Phase D the gap-analysis.

When that's done, we could summarise our revised version of the ADM as follows:

- **Phase A**: Define business-scope, business-purpose and future time-horizon(s) for the iteration; scope also identifies respective stakeholders and applicable governance for assessment and any probable implementation phases
- **Phase B**: Identify the baseline (what is already known in the architecture-repositories about the scope), then assess in more depth the 'as-is' context (adding content to the repositories as we do so)
- **Phase C**: Repeat Phase B for the one or more 'to-be' time-horizons specified in Phase A
- **Phase D**: Do a gap-analysis for each 'as-is' and 'to-be' pair (from Phase B and C respectively), to identify requirements,

constraints, risks, opportunities and suchlike for future change.

- **Phase E**: Review the results of Phase D to allocate priorities to requirements and identify appropriate means to implement the requisite changes ('solutions', in classic IT-speak); the applicable governance-rules shift from those of architecture to those of change-management during this phase
- **Phase F**: Establish a detailed plan for project-, programme- or portfolio-management to handle the changes 'from here to there' - in particular, dealing with the 'people' and 'preparation' aspects of change
- **Phase G**: Architecture assists change-governance with compliance, consistency and inter-project synergies during implementation of the planned business change
- **Phase H**: Return to architecture-governance to do a 'lessons-learned' review in relation to the respective business context, and identify any needs for further related architecture work.

> As with the Zachman-like framework that underpins it, this restructure of the TOGAF ADM is described in more detail in *Bridging the Silos*, in the 'Methodology' chapters. There's also a two-page summary of the methodology at tetradianbooks.com/ebook/silos_real-ea-adm-ref.pdf.

From this, *every* architecture iteration has the same overall structure. All that really changes is the scope, and the purpose for the iteration: once that's set up in Phase A, the rest of the activities follow on naturally from that. The 'Preliminary Phase' is actually an architecture iteration in which the scope is the architecture-capability itself. And technically speaking, Phase H is also an architecture iteration in its own right, where the scope is the current context of the architecture: but it's simplest to leave it where it is, if only to remind us to review the architecture itself on a regular basis.

> Crucially, anything that looks like content or activities for a later phase is deliberately held back until that phase. For example, we don't try to do implementation during architecture-assessment, because the applicable governance-rules are usually different in the respective phases. If we did try to do implementation too early, we'd be likely to do it wrong, or at the least annoy some important stakeholder who should have been involved!
>
> This especially applies to any pre-packaged 'solutions': anything that looks like a 'solution' is explicitly shelved until Phase E at the earliest, so that we fully understand the real requirements in the context *before* we look at any purported 'solutions' to those requirements. The aim

here is to reduce the incidence of *deus ex machina* delusions – such as the classic cart-before-the-horse mistake of 'IT-solution looking for business-problem' – that so often cause so much bitter contention with the wider business community.

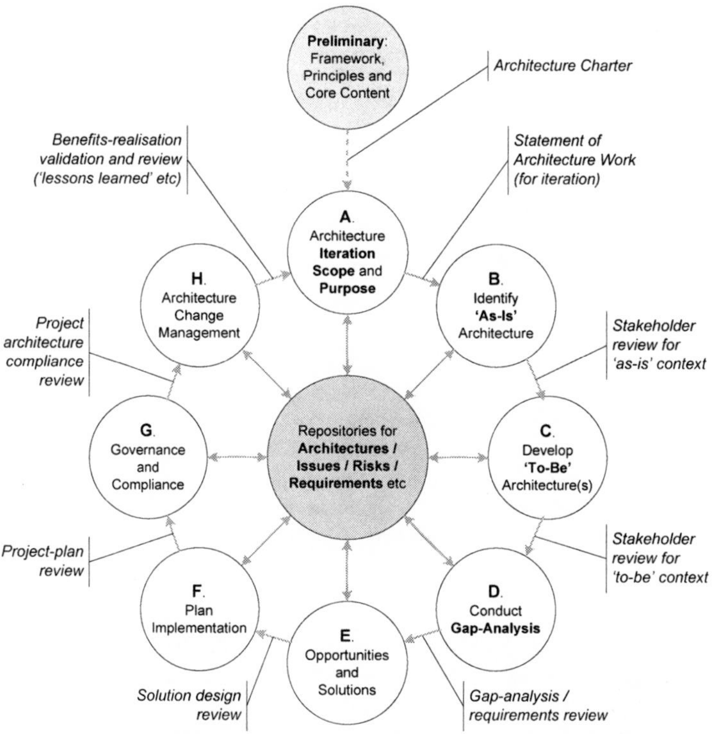

Governance-artefacts define architecture-cycle's phase-boundaries

The other advantage of this redesign is that it simplifies the link to governance. Each phase now ends with an explicit stakeholder-review: in effect, the reviews define the phase-boundaries. And the review itself provides a PRINCE2-style 'go/no-go' gateway at the end of each phase: so we don't assume - as classic TOGAF does - that every enterprise-architecture assessment must automatically lead to a major 'roadmap' for all-out change of the IT-systems. Often there's real business-value to be gained just from the assessment itself.

This is especially true once we acknowledge Dave Snowden's dictum that 'every intervention is a diagnostic, and every diagnostic is an intervention': the *process* of architecture itself – above all, the engagement in dialogue – is often the only direct 'intervention' we need.

> If you really want to cut costs, improve efficiency, enhance overall effectiveness, often the best way to do this is to get people to re-think their own way of working – not impose a 'new way of working' on them from outside. Enhanced awareness of the way in which everything links with everything else leads to small changes in action that can snowball by themselves into *natural* larger-scale change: and if we do it right, it hardly costs anything at all.

Another source of business-value is that, once we link the architecture information-repositories more strongly into the assessment methodology, even the smallest iteration will add a little more into the 'holograph', that body of knowledge about enterprise structure and purpose. This not only includes models and other architecture information, but requirements in general, updates to the shared enterprise glossary and thesaurus, and notes on new and revised risks and opportunities.

> That perhaps doesn't sound much, but even small updates to the thesaurus, for example, can help a lot, if sometimes in unexpected ways. Misunderstandings and miscommunications can cost a great deal, and not just in direct monetary terms: that thesaurus will *matter*.
>
> And opportunities can arise in some very unexpected places. The most intensive users of early mobile phones were not in the upper echelons of big-business – as the telcos had expected – but jobbing builders and small-traders, for whom communications on-site and on the move had a very high value indeed. And in those same early days, engineers would often exchange test-messages with each other via the technology's parallel control-channel, which usually worked even when there wasn't enough signal for the normal voice-channel to operate. The technique seemed useful, so, as a small experiment, one telco made the channel visible on their subscribers' handsets – and was taken completely by surprise when what's now known as 'texting' took off like wildfire. That's why text-messages are restricted to 160 characters: the control-channel wasn't designed for texting at all. But it's a clever re-use of existing technology – leading to a very valuable business opportunity.

The other point here is that by linking review of the repositories into the architecture cycle, they should never go out of date – because they're re-assessed and updated every time we do any work in the respective space.

Historically, enterprise architecture frameworks have been great on the theory, but often not so great on the practice. So there's also a lot about methodology that we can learn from other disciplines, above all on the links between knowledge, governance and action. Two valuable sources in this are ITIL – especially Version 3, which is far less IT-specific than the previous version – and PMBOK, the

'Project Management Body of Knowledge'. Another well-known example is Christopher Alexander's work on patterns in building-architecture, which has been adapted to many other architectural domains. But there are plenty of other sources for good ideas: all we need do is keep our eyes open, and remember always to think wider than just the usual constraints of the IT-centric world.

Performance – metrics

What's the value of your architecture? And value to whom? These aren't trivial questions: if you can't answer them, and if you can't prove the value, it'll likely be your job that's on the line...

There are actually four different yet interdependent themes here:

- identifying what 'value' means within in the enterprise - in other words, not just money, but all the other 'pervasives' too;
- identifying the metrics and transforms needed to measure and monitor business-activity and business-performance in terms of each of those values;
- identifying and measuring the impact that the enterprise-architecture has on those measured values - which gives us the business-value of the architecture;
- monitoring and measuring the performance of the architecture practice - just like any other business capability.

None of these are as simple as they might at first seem - though measuring the business-value of the architecture is probably the hardest challenge, because some impacts are identifiable only in terms of what *didn't* happen, what *didn't* go wrong, and often the real returns can be measured only in the performance of the enterprise as a whole.

> Oddly enough, metrics and business-value are hardly addressed at all in the TOGAF specification. You'll find more detail, though, in the 'Completion' chapters in *Bridging the Silos*, whilst the role of the 'pervasives' is explored in depth in another companion book, *The Service Oriented Enterprise* – see the *Resources* section for more information on those.

One of the hardest parts - which is why we need to address it right from the start - will be weaning people away from an over-dependence on measuring performance only in monetary terms. Whether we think of it in the positive, as profit - in a commercial enterprise - or negative, as cost-cutting - such as in a government-department - money is, obviously, an interesting and important metric. But oddly, it's often not much *use* as a metric, because very few things are directly controlled *by* money. Technically speaking, it's more usually a complex derivative, an *outcome* of other factors rather than a driver in its own right: and what we most need to measure are the things we *can* control.

> A perhaps useful piece of historical trivia here: the word 'economy' literally translates as 'the management of the household', in fact up until the middle of the nineteenth century the word 'economist' was essentially synonymous with 'housewife'. Then a few folks came up with the metaphor of an enterprise or a whole nation as a 'household' on a larger scale – and hence 'the economy' as the management of that shared 'household'. Hence, in turn, all the present-day notions of 'economics'.
>
> But in doing so, they made a fundamental mistake: they measured that economy only in monetary terms, and ignored everything else. If you do that, the 'economy' metaphor no longer works: managing the household finances is rarely easy – but in many ways it's the *easy* part of managing a household, and it's certainly not the only one!

Balanced Scorecard is a good start, to get people thinking wider than money: but even that still places financial return as one of its four dimensions, placing it on an equal footing with 'Customer', 'Internal Business Processes' and 'Innovation and Learning'. This is misleading because, unlike the others, financial return is not a lead-indicator but a lag-indicator - it tells us where we've been, but not where we're going. To manage an enterprise - or for that matter the architecture of that enterprise - what we need are those lead-indicators.

Which is where the values of the enterprise - its 'pervasives' - come into the picture, because by definition they're the themes that are of value *to* the enterprise, and hence the things we most need to measure. Which is why we need to identify them as early as possible within our enterprise-architecture work - see 'Vision, values, principles and purpose' in *Step 1: Know your business*, p.31. As a very minimum, we need to measure against those five strands of effectiveness:

- Is it *efficient*? - does it make the best use of the available resources?
- Is it *reliable*? - can it be relied on the deliver the required results?
- Is it *elegant*? - does it support the human factors in the context?

- Is it *appropriate*? – does it align with the business values and purpose?
- Is it *integrated*? – does it help to link everything together?

Once we have those, and a real 'balanced scorecard' that's tailored to the true values of the enterprise, we have a means to measure the value of the architecture.

We also need to monitor our own performance in doing enterprise architecture. Again, a focus on those five strands of effectiveness will be helpful here, but probably the best approach will be to use one of the 'capability maturity models' that are becoming more generally available for enterprise architecture.

> Two maturity-metrics that I've found useful are Marlies van Steenbergen's 'DyA Architecture Maturity Matrix', from her book *Building an Enterprise Architecture Practice*, and the Meta Group's 'Architecture Maturity Audit'. Even though they're aimed primarily at IT-architecture, they're sufficiently detailed and fine-grained enough to give valuable pointers for any type of enterprise architecture – though in my experience the Meta Group's version is the more useful of the two for assessing the early stages of architecture maturity.
>
> To keep things simple, though, we'll stick with the minimalist maturity model from the TOGAF specification for the rest of this book, as its basic five-step frame fits better with our more generic needs here. It doesn't measure performance as such, but it does provide clear guidance as to what to do next at each step – which is, after all, the real purpose of performance-metrics.

The other key aspect of performance is about lessons learned from the previous 'perform*ing*' of the work. Enterprise architecture manages a body of knowledge about enterprise structure and purpose: what have we added to that body of knowledge during this cycle of work? To quote the US Army's 'After Action Review' process:

- What was supposed to happen?
- What actually happened?
- What was the source of each difference?
- What can we learn from this, to do differently next time?

Keeping track of 'the numbers' will help – no doubt about that. But it's questions like those above, extending the *narrative* and dialogue of the architecture, that will really help most to embed the architecture into the enterprise, and to demonstrate in direct, everyday practice the real value of our work.

Resources

- FEAF (Federal Enterprise Architecture Framework): see www.gao.gov/special.pubs/eaguide.pdf [PDF]
- Preparation for enterprise IT-architecture: see Chapter 6 'Preliminary Phase' and Chapter 7 'Phase A: Architecture Vision' in Open Group, *TOGAF™ Version 9* (Van Haren, 2009)
- Architecture Development Method (ADM): see Parts II and III in online TOGAF 9 at www.opengroup.org/architecture/togaf9-doc/arch/
- DyA (Dynamic Architecture): see eng.dya.info/Home/
- Effectiveness in whole-of-enterprise architecture: see Tom Graves, *Real Enterprise Architecture: beyond IT to the whole enterprise* (Tetradian, 2008)
- ITIL (IT Infrastructure Library): see www.itil-officialsite.com
- COBIT (Control Objectives in Information and related Technology): see www.isaca.org/cobit
- PRINCE2 (Projects In Controlled Environments): see www.ogc.gov.uk/methods_prince_2.asp
- Zachman Framework: see www.zifa.com
- Framework and method for Agile architecture: see Tom Graves, *Bridging the Silos: enterprise architecture for IT-architects* (Tetradian, 2008)
- PMBOK (Project Management Body of Knowledge): see Project Management Institute at www.pmi.org and Wikipedia summary at en.wikipedia.org/wiki/Project_Management_Body_of_Knowledge
- Patterns: see Christopher Alexander, *A Pattern Language: towns, buildings, construction* (Oxford University Press, 1977)
- Balanced Scorecard and its variants: see Wikipedia summary at en.wikipedia.org/wiki/Balanced_scorecard
- Architecture maturity model: see Martin van den Berg and Marlies van Steenbergen, *Building an Enterprise Architecture Practice: tools, tips, best practices, ready-to-use insights* (Sogeti / Springer Verlag, 2006)
- Meta Group Architecture Maturity Audit: *Meta Group Practice,* (2000), Vol 4 No.4 (for Part 1) and No.5 (for Part 2)
- After Action Review and other 'lessons learned' techniques: see Chris Collison and Geoff Parcell, *Learning to Fly: practical lessons from one of the world's leading knowledge companies* (Capstone, 2001)

A MATTER OF MATURITY

What we need to do at each step in enterprise-architecture depends to a large extent on the level of maturity that's been achieved to date. The TOGAF specification describes five distinct levels that it labels 'ad-hoc', 'repeatable', 'defined', 'managed' and 'optimised'. Those, though, are the maturity-levels we achieve *after* we've done the work. The typical steps for the work itself would be more as follows:

1. From nothing, to creating a stable base for 'ad-hoc' fixes – see *Step 1: Know your business*, p.31
2. From 'ad-hoc', to structures that are efficient, reliable and repeatable – see *Step 2: Clean up the mess*, p.65
3. From repeatable, to sufficiently well defined to respond to the changing needs of strategy – see *Step 3: Strategy and stuff*, p.93
4. From defined, to managed well enough to respond in real-time to the confusions and crises coming up from the real world – see *Step 4: Work with the real world*, p.123
5. From managed, to optimised well enough to tackle the organisation's more intractable 'pain-points' and 'wicked problems' – see *Step 5: Powering on*, p.141

These layers build on each other, but the work of each layer never actually ends: we need to continue to revisit the respective context and scope for each, to review and amend as we climb upward.

(Start EA dev'ment)
Level 1: **Ad-hoc**
Level 2: **Repeatable**
Level 3: **Defined**
Level 4: **Managed**
Level 5: **Optimised**
Maintain the dialogue
Step 5: **Powering on** (spiral-out assessment)
Step 4: **Work with the real world** (bottom-up assessment)
Step 3: **Strategy and stuff** (top-down assessment)
Step 2: **Clean up the mess** (horizontal assessment)
Step 1: **Know your business** (focus on business-purpose)

Continuing updates for each layer underpin maturity growth

So if and when we get to the 'Optimised' maturity-level, there'll always still be further work to do, in maintaining the dialogue that underpins the architecture - see *What next?*, p.165. But at least we know we'll be doing it from strong, stable foundations - and contributing in every way towards real business value.

Resources

- 🕮 Levels of architecture maturity in TOGAF: see chapter 51, 'Architecture Maturity Models' in The Open Group, *TOGAF™ Version 9* (Van Haren, 2009)
- TOGAF (The Open Group Architecture Framework): see www.opengroup.org/architecture/togaf9-doc/arch/

STEP 1: KNOW YOUR BUSINESS

We can only implement a strategy successfully if we have *some* initial idea about what business we're in. IT-oriented 'enterprise architects' often try to skip this step in the rush to get down to 'the fun stuff' - the fine detail of computing technology. But it can be a lethal mistake, because we end up optimising the technology for a business that we don't even know - and hence are then all but forced into the trap of promoting pre-packaged IT-'solutions' *as* strategies, because it's the only part of the business we *do* know. So, to put it simply:

**Whatever part of the business we're in,
the business of the business must always come first.**

Which means that however much we might want to 'get down and get dirty' with the detail-level IT - which usually is the next stage, by the way - we *must* do this task first.

Purpose and strategy: The focus here is on the nature of the business - its vision, values and business purpose, the business milieu in which it operates and its role within that context, and its core business functions and processes.

Our aim here is to show *why* an architecture capability would be useful for the enterprise - and demonstrate that use by producing, at minimal cost, a simple set of architectural artefacts that have immediate practical value for the business.

> From a FEAF perspective, what we're creating here is a first cut at the BRM and PRM – the Business Reference Model and Performance Reference Model.
>
> From a TOGAF perspective, much of what happens here would be termed 'Business Architecture'. But note that we do much of it *before* we develop the Architecture Charter and the like: in fact much of the equivalent of TOGAF's Preliminary Phase happens near the end of this stage, rather than at the start. The reason is simple business-politics: yes, we must do all the Preliminary Phase work before we get down to what TOGAF thinks of as 'enterprise architecture' – but we won't even get that far unless we already have some business credibility behind us. Which means we need to do something that is immediately meaningful and valuable to the everyone in the business – not just the IT-types. Hence the slightly back-to-front way we'll do things here.
>
> We still do it under solid governance, though – stakeholder reviews and all that. Unless we do that, it isn't *architecture*.

People and governance: This is only a first-cut 'proof of concept', so we'll need to keep things as simple as possible. Often it'll be slipped in 'under the counter' as a kind of skunk-works project, with costs quietly buried under someone's discretionary budget - though for credibility reasons it'd be best if that 'someone' is fairly senior to start with. In governance terms, that 'someone' would also be who we would report to during the work, though the end-results - the Function Model, the Architecture Charter and so on - should be distributed for comment as widely as possible.

> This is one of the few parts of enterprise-architecture that could be done entirely by external consultants or other 'outsiders'. In fact it's almost better to use outsiders here, especially in the early stages, because they would see the enterprise differently from any 'insider's assumptions, and would also have more licence to ask the essential 'stupid questions' such as "What *is* this business, anyway?".

Planning and frameworks: We have a minor dilemma here, in that whilst we're aiming to create the core overviews of the enterprise, the 'holograph' approach means we need one already existing before we can start, so as to derive business value. The answer is to use the Zachman-like framework described earlier in 'Planning - frameworks', in *Preparing for architecture* (p.13), as it provides a core taxonomy to make sense of where and how everything fits together. Ultimately, everything we'll do from now on will anchor back into that core framework: so we don't just end up with an enterprise architecture, we start with one.

> You will also need a fairly complete architecture toolset: architecture repository and framework, requirements repository, risks and opportunities registers, and preferably the glossary and thesaurus as well. (You won't need the dispensations register as yet, because we don't get that far in this stage.)
>
> But whilst it does have to be fairly complete, it doesn't need to be that sophisticated as yet. For the first pass through this work, you *can* get away with using standard office applications such as Excel, PowerPoint and Visio. This would also be good as a test-case for a trial version of a proper purpose-built toolset – but do first make sure that you *can* export from the toolset, otherwise you risk losing all of this work.

Practice and methods: Each section of work should follow the standard method and governance as described earlier in 'Practice - methods', in *Preparing for architecture* (p.20). The only variation would be that in some sections, such as developing the Function Model - see 'Functions and services' below (p.48) - it may be useful to do the 'to-be' (Phase C) before the 'as-is' (Phase B), to help stakeholders disengage from assumptions about the imagined 'inevitability' of current organisational structures and processes.

Although it's unlikely there would be much – if any – design and implementation for formal change-projects to do here, it will still be important to engage programme-management and the like in the overall process – if only to garner their suggestions and feed-back on how the handovers of governance-responsibilities will need to work when we move later into the more active stages of enterprise architecture.

Performance, end-products and metrics: First time through, the overall work for this step should require no more than a few person-weeks of effort – just enough to establish the intended role and business value of the architecture capability. You'll probably need to take more time when you revisit this work at later stages of maturity, but that above should be sufficient to make a useful start here. Typical artefacts from this step would include:

- strategic description of the enterprise context – vision, values, purpose, market, legal and regulatory milieu, etc
- high-level descriptions of the needs within that context that are serviced by the organisation
- core content for the architecture framework – assets, functions, locations, capabilities, events and decisions
- core Function Model – 'the enterprise on a page' – summarising how the organisation serves those needs
- formal documentation of the authorised roles, responsibilities, activities, deliverables, funding and reporting-relationships for the enterprise architecture capability

This step would usually be run as an explicit short-term project, hence key metrics would typically include on-time, on-budget, and all required deliverables completed. Also some measure of customer-satisfaction would be useful – not only satisfaction of direct customers such as the project-sponsor, but more generally of the likely architecture stakeholders.

Vision, values, principles and purpose

At the highest level, 'the enterprise' is not the organisation, but the broader context in which the organisation operates, and which it shares with all other stakeholders in that enterprise. The ***purpose*** of this section is to identify and document the organisation's relationships with that broader enterprise.

> You'll also find this type of assessment useful as part of due-diligence for a proposed merger or acquisition. Assuming you've already done this for your own organisation, this exercise will provide you with the essential information for a gap-analysis on culture and background – the basis for a crucial go/no-go decision, because the degree of alignment is a known key criterion for future success or failure here.

On the ***people*** side, the skills you'll need are those for routine business-analysis. For a first pass you'll probably only need to meet up with a few strategists and other senior players, though for later iterations you'll need to extend that scope, eventually to every part and every level of the overall enterprise.

For ***planning***, you'll need access to typical business documentation such as the Annual Report and the corporate intranet. The architecture-entities you identify will usually be placed in the topmost rows of the framework.

The ***practice*** would be based on techniques such as visioning and the Business Motivation Model, with appropriate documentation.

As described above, ***performance*** would usually be measured in simple project-completion terms: on-time, on-budget and suchlike.

Vision, role, mission, goal

Use the 'vision, role, mission, goal' structure to summarise the overall ecosystem in which the organisation exists, and the role or roles it chooses to play within that ecosystem.

> Note that the terms 'vision' and 'mission' are used here in a slightly different way than in common business use – see the Glossary on p.180 for definitions. These usages help us to avoid the temptation to view the organisation *as* the enterprise – one of the most common yet most dangerous mistakes in business-visioning.
>
> For more detail on the 'vision, role, mission, goal' process, see the chapter 'Architecture on purpose' in *Real Enterprise Architecture: beyond IT to the whole enterprise*, and the 'Practice – Service Purpose' chapter in *The Service Oriented Enterprise: enterprise architecture and viable services*.

The vision is not a 'future state' for the organisation itself, but describes the common theme shared by *all* stakeholders in the enterprise. The typical phrasing of a vision would not be emotive in itself, but would invite or incite an emotional commitment to the shared 'cause': two good examples are "a sociable world" (brewers Lion Nathan) and "boundaryless information flow" (standards-body The Open Group). A mission here is more in the sense of a trade-mission, not a military-style 'sending' – in other words, an ongoing *capability* to serve a role within the enterprise, rather than an activity with a defined point of completion.

- What **vision** is common to all stakeholders in the enterprise? What single phrase *describes* the overall enterprise?
- What **role** or roles does the organisation play within the enterprise, to contribute towards the vision? What roles does it *not* play - hence leaving open for other stakeholders? Who are these other stakeholders, and what roles do *they* play within the overall enterprise? What relationships and transactions are implied by these different roles within the enterprise? How would you verify that each role - especially the organisation's own chosen role or roles - does support the enterprise vision?
- What **mission** or missions - ongoing services and capabilities - would be needed to support each role undertaken by the organisation in that enterprise? What metrics would you need to confirm that each mission is 'on purpose' and *effective* in supporting the respective role?
- What short-, medium- and longer-term **goals** and objectives underpin each mission? What are the timescales and deliverables for each goal? By what means do you verify that each goal is achievable, and has been achieved? How do you verify that each goal does support the respective mission in an appropriate and effective way?

Once this basic high-level picture has been established, use a technique such as the Business Motivation Model to devolve the view downward into the detailed operations of the organisation.

> Beware, though, that the BMM does tend towards that dangerous self-referential notion of organisation as 'the enterprise' – particularly in its handling of higher-level terms such as 'vision' and 'mission'. Remember that the real enterprise here is *always* larger than the organisation: the detail-layers of the BMM work well enough, but take care at the top!

Store the results in the architecture-repository either in row-0 (for the vision and role, which should probably never change) or in the upper rows of the 'reason/decision' column (for missions and goals). Also note any additional information requirements, risks and opportunities that may arise, and save these to the respective repositories.

Values

Next, identify the required, espoused and actual **values** indicated for the organisation's relationships in the enterprise:

- What shared values are required from every player in the overall enterprise, in order for that enterprise to achieve success within the terms of its vision?
- What individual and collective values - either implicit or explicit - are required to support each of the relationships and transactions in the organisation's roles within the enterprise?
- What values does the organisation espouse, both in its relationships with others and its relationships within and to itself?
- What actual values does the organisation express in its actions and relations with others and within itself?
- Are there are any misalignments between required, espoused and actual values? If so, what impacts do these differences have, on the effectiveness of the shared enterprise, of the organisation in relation to and with the enterprise, and the organisation's internal function and relationships within itself?

Identify required values from an assessment of what 'effectiveness' would look like in relation to the enterprise and its vision: for example, fairness and trust will usually be required in almost any functional enterprise.

Identify espoused values from the organisation's Annual Report or other public sources, such as an 'About Us' or 'Our Values' section on a website, or publicity material provided to prospective employees.

Identify actual values from the behaviours or phrases actually used within the organisation; note especially how these may vary at different levels or in different parts of the organisation.

> The SEMPER diagnostic can be valuable here, because it's designed to identify the effective 'ability to do work' from the kind of language used to describe different aspects of the work-context. If the organisation claims that it values transparency, for example, yet people are using phrases such as "we're just mushrooms, fed sh*t and kept in the dark", it does kind of imply there's a significant mismatch between espoused and actual values! In some organisations, the scale of mismatch can be *huge* – with correspondingly huge impacts on the organisation's overall effectiveness, too...

A SEMPER analysis can be downright scary at times, because of the ease with which it surfaces problematic issues such as those value-mismatches; but it does also describe what to do to resolve each of those problems. You'll find more detail on SEMPER in the book *SEMPER and SCORE*, and also on the sempermetrics.com website.

Document the required and espoused values in the uppermost rows of the architecture framework, and also as core requirements in the requirements repository. Document each values-mismatch as a priority item in the risks register.

Principles

From values we move to **principles**, because the organisation's principles describe how its values should be expressed in practice. Values define the 'pervasives' for the enterprise, but in themselves are somewhat abstract; whereas principles are - or should be - concrete, actionable and verifiable.

One key complication is that, by their nature, principles will often compete or conflict: transparency versus privacy, for example, or innovation versus the safety of 'the known'. We need to document such clashes, and, wherever practicable, assign priority to one or other principle so as to simplify decision-making in the field.

One useful principle, perhaps, is an acknowledgement that although every person in the enterprise is personally responsible for resolving the balance of principles, no-one ever actually achieves it – not in the real world, anyway!

The appropriate test there would not be a demand for an impossible 'perfection', but more that all applicable principles were taken into account, and that all reasonable efforts were made to resolve any conflicts, under the constraints of the context.

Principles are not law as such, but in some ways are almost *above* the law – they're what law is drawn from, in fact. Law describes how things *ought* to work in theory; principles provide guidance as to how to make things work in practice. In effect, a law is a pre-packaged interpretation of principles: so whenever we meet a circumstance where 'the law' – in the enterprise sense, as the organisation's rule-book or whatever – doesn't make practical sense, we need to recognise the primacy of the underlying principles.

That's why the first principle in the TOGAF specification is about the primacy of principles: principles really do come first. But they in turn express the enterprise values; and the values themselves express the shared vision that defines what the enterprise *is*. That's why all this perhaps abstract-seeming stuff *matters*: because without it, the organisation has no practical purpose. Which is *not* a good idea...

Principles form hierarchies as they devolve down into the deeper detail. But ultimately every one of them needs to be anchored back into one or more values; and in turn every value needs to be expressed in explicit, measurable, actionable principles:

- What principles apply in the enterprise? In what ways are these principles expressed and documented?
- What value or values does each principle express? How would you confirm that those values are expressed by the principles?
- Are there any principles - explicit or implicit - that do *not* seem to be anchored in any espoused enterprise value? If so, what values are implied by such principles? Do any such 'shadow' values conflict with the espoused values of the organisation? If so, how, and which values 'win'?
- What principles express each value? Is every espoused value expressed within at least one hierarchy of principles which devolves all the way down to the operations layer? If not, what principles would be required to express that value?
- In what ways are each principle applied, in theory, and in practice? What evidence exists that they *are* applied? - or not applied? If not applied in practice, what needs to be done to ensure that they *are* applied? What metrics would be needed to monitor and confirm this?
- What conflicts exists between principles? What guidance is provided to help people resolve such conflicts between principles in their own work?

For a first pass at this in an 'architecture demonstrator' project, you would probably only assess this at the most abstract level; but in later reviews you'll need to go much deeper, sometimes right down to the fine detail of system design and everyday operations. It's only when values are expressed as principles that they become meaningful *as* values: until then they're just an abstract 'nice idea'.

> The TOGAF 9 specification includes a very useful section – Chapter 23, 'Architecture Principles' – about principles and how to define and document them. As usual, we'll need to compensate for TOGAF's obsessive IT-centrism – such as its bizarre assertion that architecture principles are a subset of IT-principles – but otherwise their recommended format for defining principles works well in any context:
>
> - *name*: represents the essence of the rule in a form that is easy to remember;
> - *statement*: presents a succinct, unambiguous summary of the rule;

- *rationale*: anchors the principle back to the business reasons and business-benefits arising from the principle, and ultimately to the core value or values that it represents;
- *implications*: describes how the principle should be expressed in everyday actions or in influence on practical decisions.

"Essentially, principles drive behaviour", says the TOGAF specification. It also adds a checklist of keywords for validating well-described principles: *understandable, robust, complete, consistent* and *stable*; to these we should also add *measurable* and *verifiable*, so that we have some means to confirm that the principle has been applied n practice. Recommended, anyway.

Principles represent the core reasons and decisions of the organisation, pervading the values throughout every layer and function, downward into the fine detail of systems designs and individual actions. Document them in the respective rows of the 'decisions' column of the framework and in the requirements repository, as linked trails of decomposition and derivation linked back to the root enterprise-value.

Business purpose

Finally, as a crosscheck, we come back to **purpose**. The previous parts of the assessment should have identified what the organisation believes its business purpose to be; we now need to check that against the reality. The difference can sometimes be painful, but nonetheless important to know…

Our guide for this is a phrase coined by the cyberneticist Stafford Beer: "the purpose of a system is what it does". In systems-theory terms, the organisation is a system in its own right, interacting with the larger ecosystem of the overall enterprise. The vision, values and principles define what the organisation's purpose *should* be, in theory; Beer's phrase - usually shown as its acronym 'POSIWID' - indicates its effective purpose in practice, and hence the *actual* principles, values and, probably, vision.

The organisation states that health and safety are key values, but the reality is that there are high rates of accidents, illness and absenteeism. From POSIWID, we can be fairly certain that those themes are *not* valued in practice…

The organisation's websites asserts the primacy of quality above everything else in its products. But POSIWID shows us that the managers believe the only thing that matters is 'the numbers' – and their bonuses reflect that fact, too. Notice what impact this has on product-quality – and on overall effectiveness…

> Values *matter*: yet we need to be clear which values *actually* apply in the enterprise, otherwise we have no means to identify when what we do really *is* 'on purpose'.

Any values-mismatch will lead to ineffectiveness: each is something we'll need to address as an organisation – and hence needs to be documented in the architecture gap-analysis.

- If "the purpose of the system is what it does", what *real* principles and values are implied in what happens in the organisation and in its relations with the overall enterprise?
- Comparing the results with the values and principles already documented, what conflicts can be identified? In each case, do the espoused values have priority, or the actual 'shadow' values? What is the impact of each values-mismatch on overall effectiveness?

Document each mismatch of values or principles as a high-priority entry in the risks-register.

The enterprise context

The ***purpose*** of this section is to establish the context and expectations of the overall enterprise in which the organisation operates. This includes concerns such as legal and regulatory constraints, applicable industry and other standards, and the key 'things', locations and events that comprise the enterprise context.

On the ***people*** side, the skills you'll need, as in the previous section, are those for routine business-analysis. You'll also need access to a handful of 'insiders' who know the nature of the business fairly well – which could be you, of course.

For ***planning***, most of the information you'll need would be provided by those 'insiders': you *could* find it by slogging your way through documents and intranets and industry reference-material, but asking the right people a few questions will be much quicker! The aim here is to populate more of the framework's upper rows, so you'll need some kind of architecture repository, as before.

The ***practice*** would be based on standard business-analysis techniques, documented as described below.

As before, ***performance*** would be measured in simple project-completion terms, reporting back to the project sponsor.

Compliance, constraints, standards, expectations

In the previous section we'll have identified the overall milieu - the 'vision' - and the role that the organisation plays within it, which identifies the effective requirements. In aligning itself to the vision, the organisation *chooses* concomitant constraints implied by its values and principles. Here we explore the constraints that come in to the organisation *from* the milieu, by dint of choosing to enact that role within the enterprise. These include any laws and other regulations that would apply; any required standards from the industry, or needed for interaction with customers, suppliers, partners and other players in the enterprise; and expectations from the general community about corporate social responsibility and the like.

These constraints will each have differing degrees of 'bindedness', and may vary in different jurisdictions, geographies, communities and so on:

- What laws and other regulations apply in this business context? To what extent and in what ways are they binding on the organisation? In what ways do these vary in differing jurisdictions and the like?
- What constraints - and opportunities - do these imply for the organisation and its business in the enterprise? What trade-offs do these imply against the business requirements?
- By what means would the business confirm its compliance with these constraints? What actions and information would be required? How would you monitor and measure compliance? What would be the consequences of failure to comply? What opportunities arise from the required compliance with these constraints?

> Note that these can be a lot more complicated than they may at first seem: some regulations are binding across geographies, and some jurisdictions assert their reach into other contexts entirely. US regulations on technology export or money-laundering, for example, are deemed to apply throughout the entire supply-chain from source to end-user. And movement of staff may be restricted not only by local residency-rules, but also some very nasty booby-traps such as the way some countries extend their citizen-obligations to foreign-born children of former nationals. The definition of 'former national' can be dangerously blurry here, as one of our colleagues discovered the hard way in Greece after moving there on business: although he'd been born in Australia, and a full Australian citizen, the fact that one of his grandparents had been Greek meant he was also classed as a Greek citizen – and he was forcibly drafted into compulsory two-year

military-service there. Such realities are genuine risks for the globalised enterprise: we need to be aware of them in the architecture.

Such details may not matter too much on a first pass assessment, of course, but they certainly *do* matter when we explore these concerns in more depth in subsequent reviews.

Next we need to note the various standards that would apply in each context:

- What standards – quality-standards, technical standards, interface standards, language standards and suchlike – apply in each area of this business context? To what extent and in what ways are they binding on the respective areas of the organisation? In what ways do these vary in differing regions and the like?
- What constraints – and opportunities – do these imply for the organisation and its business in the enterprise? What trade-offs do these imply against the business requirements?
- By what means would the business confirm its compliance with the constraints of these standards? What actions and information would be required? How would you monitor and measure compliance? What would be the consequences of failure to comply? What opportunities arise from the required compliance with these constraints?

And there are what we might call 'good citizen' constraints, which may not have the force of law or formal standards behind them, but can still impose serious sanctions in terms of reputation or cooperation:

- What social expectations and social standards – ethics, environment, general 'good neighbourliness' and so on – apply in each area of this business context? To what extent and in what ways are they binding on the respective areas of the organisation? In what ways do these vary in differing regions and the like?
- What constraints – and opportunities – do these imply for the organisation and its business in the enterprise? What trade-offs do these imply against the business requirements?
- By what means would the business confirm its compliance with the constraints of these expectations and standards? What actions and information would be required? How would you monitor and measure compliance? What would be the consequences of failure to comply? What opportunities arise from the required compliance with these constraints?

> The SEMPER diagnostic might also be helpful here as an initial metric, identifying effective social reputation via language-cues in descriptions of the organisation from the broader community and other 'external' stakeholders.

Document the results in the respective parts of the architecture repository: the constraints themselves in the 'decisions' column of the framework, required metrics in the 'virtual asset' segment, risks and consequences in the risks-register, and so on.

Assets, locations, events

In this part of the work we aim to fill out more of the core parts of the framework, by identifying the assets, locations and events that are central to the organisation's business within the enterprise.

> There are a lot of questions in this part, many of which may seem very unfamiliar – even bizarre, perhaps – if your previous architecture experience has been only in an IT-centric context. Don't worry about it, though: all these questions and categorisations do matter, as we'll see later, but we don't have to do it all in one go! If any part seems too alien to make sense, do the best you can for now, and allow the questions to make more sense over time as this much larger picture of the enterprise starts to coalesce.
>
> Later on we'll need to go into all of this in much more depth, of course, but for a first-pass this review would need only to capture the most essential types of items – enough to create some kind of top-level anchor for subsequent iterations of the architecture cycle.

So first, assess the key **asset-types**:

- What types of *physical assets* - physical 'things' - are important to the organisation's business? What roles do these assets play in the business - for example, as input supplies, as output products, or used as consumables in business processes? What value does each type of 'thing' have for the business? How are these assets obtained, maintained, monitored, managed through their life-cycle, and disposed-of at the end of it?
- What types of *virtual assets* - data, information, knowledge - are important to the organisation's business? What roles do these assets play in the business - for example, as records, as metrics, as content for delivered services, as controls in business processes? What value does each type of virtual-asset have for the business? How are these assets created, obtained, maintained, monitored, managed through their life-cycle, and disposed-of at the end of it?

- What types of *relational assets* – relationships with other organisations and actual people – are important to the organisation's business? What roles do these assets play in the business – for example, as links with employees, suppliers, customers, shareholders, regulatory bodies, other stakeholders? How are these links used in business processes – such as through contracts and other agreements? What value does each type of relational-asset have for the business? By what means does the organisation identify when relational-assets need to be created, or have been changed, damaged or deleted, by the entity at the 'far end' of the link? How are these assets obtained, maintained, monitored and managed through their life-cycle?
- What types of *aspirational assets* – the personal sense of belonging, commitment and shared-purpose – are important to the organisation's business? In what ways do others connect to the business – for example, morale and commitment of employees, customers' sense of 'belonging' via a brand, or community perception of reputation? To what does the organisation itself belong – for example, to a nation, to an industry, or to the shared enterprise as represented by its vision and role? What impacts do these assets have in business processes such as in HR, productivity, marketing? What value does each type of aspirational-asset have for the business? By what means does the organisation identify when aspirational-assets need to be created, or have been changed, damaged or deleted, by the entity at the 'far end' of the link? How are these assets obtained, maintained, monitored and managed through their life-cycle?
- What types of other *abstract assets* – abstract conceptual entities such as finance, credit and energy – are important to the organisation's business? What roles do these assets play in the business – for example, as access to resources for business processes, as measures of success, as relational factors in transactions? What value does each type of abstract-asset have for the business? How are these assets obtained, maintained, monitored and managed through their life-cycle?

Document each type in the upper rows of the respective segment of the 'assets' column in the framework.

> In business we would often talk about assets and liabilities as if they're different things. But in architectural terms they're actually the same: a

'liability' is an asset that has been assigned a negative value, or is a future promise to deliver that asset.. So if you come across references to liabilities, document them as if they're the respective type of asset, but with a rider to indicate the negative valuation.

Finally, some asset-types will only make sense as composites: a paper form, for example, is a combination of physical asset (paper) and virtual-asset (information-record). Wherever practicable, we need to be able to split these into their base-categories, to enable down-to-the-roots redesigns in the more difficult architecture concerns such as disaster-recovery planning; but in some cases such decompositions may not make any sense, and we'll need to document that fact:

- What types of *composite assets* – combinations of any of the above 'atomic' asset-categories – are important to the organisation's business? What are their base asset-categories? In what ways is it possible – or not possible, in practice – to split the composite into its base-categories? What are the consequences of *not* being able to split the composite into its base-categories?

Document each of these as a composite that bridges the respective segments of the 'assets' column.

Next, assess the key types of **location** and their composites:

- What types of *physical locations* and their associated location-schemas – geographic, building-floor etc – are important to the organisation's business? What roles do these locations play in the business – for example, as retail contact-points, manufacturing locations, physical storage, resource sites? What value does each type of location have for the business? How are these locations identified, obtained, maintained, monitored, and managed through their life-cycle?
- What types of *virtual locations* and their associated location-schemas – networks, naming, web-addresses, contact-numbers etc – are important to the organisation's business? What roles do these locations play in the business – for example, as virtual contact-points, as nodes for information routes? What value does each type of virtual-location have for the business? How are these locations identified, created, obtained, maintained, monitored, managed through their life-cycle, and disposed-of at the end of it?
- What types of *relational locations* and their associated location-schemas – such as market-segments, nodes in reporting-

relationship trees and social-networks - are important to the organisation's business? What roles do these locations play in the business? How are these locations used in business processes? What value does each type of relational-location have for the business? By what means does the organisation identify when relational-locations need to be created, or have been damaged or deleted, by the entity at the 'far end' of the link? How are these locations identified, created, maintained, monitored and managed through their life-cycle?

- What types of *aspirational locations* and their associated location-schemas - in particular, the end-nodes of aspirational-assets - are important to the organisation's business? What value does each type of aspirational-location have for the business? How are these locations identified, maintained, monitored and managed through their life-cycle?
- What types of other *abstract locations* and their associated location-schemas - time and time-zones, for example - are important to the organisation's business? What roles do these locations play in the business - for example, as reference-points for measurement of performance? What value does each type of abstract-location have for the business? How are these locations identified, maintained, monitored and - where feasible - managed through their life-cycle?
- What types of *composite locations* - combinations of any of the above 'atomic' location-categories - are important to the organisation's business? What are their base location-categories? In what ways is it possible - or not possible, in practice - to split the composite into its base-categories? What are the consequences of *not* being able to split the composite into its base-categories?

Document each type in the upper rows of the respective segment of the framework 'locations' column, or as a composite bridging the respective segments of the 'locations' column.

And assess the key categories of **events** and their composites:

- What types of *physical events* are important to the organisation's business? What roles do these events play in the business, as input- or output-triggers for routine or exceptional business processes? What value does each type of physical event have for the business? How are these events identified, monitored and managed within an overall life-cycle?

- What types of *virtual events* – messages, signals, data-values – are important to the organisation's business? What roles do these events play in the business, as input- or output-triggers for routine or exceptional business processes? What value does each type of virtual-event have for the business? How are these events identified, monitored and managed within an overall life-cycle?
- What types of *relational events* – arrivals, departures, contacts, other events in relationships with other organisations and actual people – are important to the organisation's business? What roles do these events play in the business, as input- or output-triggers for routine or exceptional business processes? What value does each type of relational-event have for the business? How are these events identified, monitored and managed within an overall life-cycle?
- What types of *aspirational events* – such as reputation- or public-relations events, or changes to brand – are important to the organisation's business? What roles do these events play in the business, as input- or output-triggers for routine or exceptional business processes? What value does each type of aspirational-event have for the business? How are these events identified, monitored and managed within an overall life-cycle?
- What types of other *abstract events* – such as cycles of time – are important to the organisation's business? What roles do these events play in the business, as input- or output-triggers for routine or exceptional business processes? What value does each type of abstract-event have for the business? How are these events identified, monitored and managed within an overall life-cycle?
- What types of *composite events* – combinations of any of the above 'atomic' event-categories – are important to the organisation's business? What are their base event-categories? In what ways is it possible – or not possible, in practice – to split the composite into its base-categories? What are the consequences of *not* being able to split the composite into its base-categories?

Document each type in the upper rows of the respective segment of the framework 'events' column, or as a composite bridging the respective segments of the 'events' column.

Functions and services

The *purpose* of this section is to establish what the organisation does, and the skills and experience needed to do it.

On the *people* side, the skills and people-contacts you'll need will be much the same as for the previous section, such as those for routine business-analysis.

For *planning*, most of the information you'll need would again come from those 'insiders'; much of it resides only in people's heads, and often you'll find you're the first person to write it all down. The aim here is to define core content for the upper rows of the remaining two framework columns, 'function' and 'capability'.

The *practice* would be based on standard business-analysis.

And *performance* would again be measured in project-completion terms, as specified by the project sponsor.

Services

For this section it's useful to take a 'service-oriented' view of the enterprise, and assert that *everything* in an enterprise delivers a service. As the ITIL v3 specification puts it, "Customers do not buy products: they buy the satisfaction of particular needs". And we satisfy those 'particular needs' through the services we provide. In that sense, products are proto-services that provide the end-customer with a means to deliver a self-service: for example, a vacuum-cleaner provides the service of cleaned floors.

This gives us a means to understand the mutual role of enterprise functions and capabilities, because a service is a structured combination of function and capability. One way to model at a high level this primacy of services is through a ***Results Logic Diagram***, which constructs a trail of derivations from the end-result of the organisation's activities - such as in the FEAF specification's term 'services to citizens' - back through the layers of internal services and their results, to the core functions of the organisation.

> A mild warning: it's very easy to misuse a Results Logic Diagram to justify the existing structure of the organisation – which may be fair enough, but that's not really the point here!
>
> What we want is a gap-analysis from 'as-is' to 'to-be', to identify potential for useful change. But if we start the Results Logic from the 'as-is', by definition there would be no gap, and hence no real point – other than as a public-relations exercise, perhaps. Instead, first do it strictly as a 'to-be' analysis: imagine that, given a perfect world, what business-functions and services would you need, to support all of the

steps in the 'results logic'? Once you have that, you can link across to the 'as-is', to develop that gap-analysis that you need.

To build the diagram, start from the enterprise vision as identified earlier:

- Given the overall priority - the vision - for the enterprise, what are the key *client-results* for the organisation's stakeholder-groups - its equivalent of 'services to citizens'?
- For each client-result, what are your respective *enterprise-results* - the measures or metrics by which the organisation confirms that it has achieved its own outcomes *and* the client outcomes?
- For each enterprise-result, what is the tree of *intermediate-results* - the linked outcomes of subsidiary Missions?
- For each set of intermediate-results, what is the *premise* - the set of core assumptions defining the role of a service-group?
- For each premise, what is the *service-group* within the organisation that delivers that service or Mission?

Given that hierarchy of results, we can then start to model the matching hierarchy of services that would deliver those results. From there, we can identify common functions that underpin the services, and the differing capabilities that actually deliver them.

Functions

The terms 'function', 'capability' and 'service' are often blurred together, but perhaps the best way to understand 'function' is to think of it in mathematical terms: a function such as $a=func(x,y)$ implies that something is returned - often in changed form - from the activity of the function. So to look for business functions, look for where something *happens* in the business - in particular, where something is changed. Services describe *what* it is that the business delivers; functions describe what it *does*.

Because of this, a ***Function Model*** is one of the most useful tools in the entire enterprise-architecture. We can use it as a single-page summary of the business *as* a whole; we can use it as a base-map for all manner of other cross-references, from project-touchpoints to costings to information-systems and process-flows; we've often seen managers use it as a way to show new recruits where their own work fits in with that of everyone else.

This is the one architecture artefact that makes immediate sense to everyone: it *matters*.

If you're looking for quick wins and instant credibility – which you usually will be, at this earliest stage of the game – then creating even a simple Function Model should be one of your highest priorities. You'll need also to have done at least some of the work above, to help you make sense of the information as an architect, but this is where other people will tend to sit up and start to take architecture seriously.

For a first-cut you'll probably only need a two-tier version, with perhaps a few hints towards the more detailed third-tier – more on that in a moment. But you should be able to get together something useful and meaningful within even a couple of days'-worth of trawling: so not only is it a valuable model, it doesn't cost much to do, either.

The model is a layered list of business functions, laid out as a visual summary of what the enterprise does. The aim here is to create a model that remains much the same as long as the organisation does that kind of work, so it needs to be independent of any current assumptions about business structure. So we start with the 'to-be' model, the description of the idealised enterprise, and then later work backwards to the 'as-is' to give us our gap-analysis.

There are no set rules about layout: the 'best' model is whatever best describes the business. Whichever way we do it, though, it's usually organised as a nested hierarchy, with three or four tiers of functions:

- *Tier 1*: major categories of business functions - key aspects of what the organisation as a whole actually *does*.
- *Tier 2*: clusters of related activities - the major support-missions for the tier-1 functions.
- *Tier 3*: 'activities' or clusters of related tasks - typically the emphasis of a team's or a person's work.
- *Tier 4*: the individual tasks within business processes - the actual delivery-processes.

There's rarely enough space on a diagram for the tier-4 functions, so they're usually listed within a supporting text document.

Some industries already have their own generic function-models, such as eTOM for telcos, and SCOR for supply-chain and logistics. They'll need adaptation to the specific context of the enterprise, even within the respective industry, but they're useful as guidelines in any case.

To identify candidate functions and activities, trawl through any available sources for information about points where business processes start and end, or wherever something is changed:

- org-chart entries: each role implies one or more business functions – though they may overlap, or be repeated in multiple locations, or aggregate several distinct functions
- the organisation's Annual Report: almost by definition, this is supposed to list every major category of business activity
- references to projects: each is likely to imply a new or upgraded capability, which again implies a function
- references to phone-lines or other contact-points: these imply business-functions behind the points of contact
- business data-models: look for the implied functions that would create, read, aggregate, update or delete the information-items

> The other obvious source for information is through conversations with appropriate staff – though beware that they're likely to want you to list every one of their tasks as a top-level business function!

Every business function *does* something, so each function-label on the model should include a verb. For tier-1 and tier-2 functions you can get away with using abstract verbs such as 'Provide' or 'Manage', but for tier-3 or tier-4 especially, you need to use more proper descriptive verbs such as 'Receive', 'Assess' or 'Monitor'.

For ***tier-1 functions***, ask:

- What are the major categories of business functions?
- How do these functions relate with each other, in terms of service-categories and service-layering?

Aim to define some six to twelve tier-1 functions. These will usually be evident in the structure of the enterprise: for example, every organisation will have a set of contact-points for customers and other stakeholders, a set of core business-processes, a layer for strategy and management, and a set of business-support functions such as HR and finance.

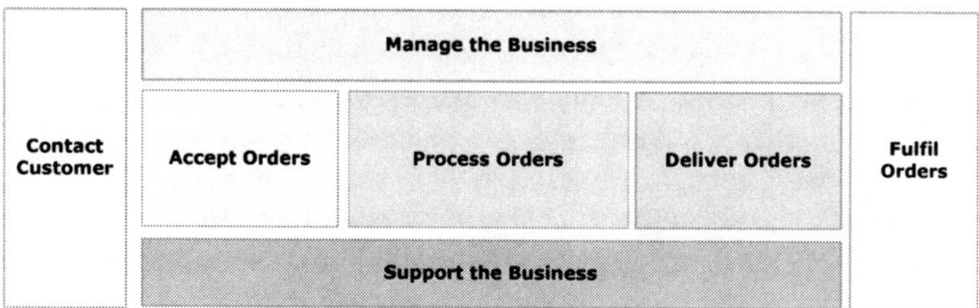

Functions: tier-1 example

Functions at tier-3 and below are relatively easy to identify in the trawl through documents and the like. But ***tier-2 functions*** are often less obvious at first, and we'll need to derive them from natural clusterings of tier-3 functions, such as implied by higher-level entries in the org-chart, or groups of functions that reappear together in different locations. So for each tier-1 category:

- What are the main clusters of related activities that occur within this category?
- How do these functions relate with each other, in terms of service-categories and service-layering?

Expect to identify around 40 to 50 of these in total. They can sometimes be found from job-titles: a truck driver, for example, or a warehouse manager, who each do a range of related business activities and tasks. The org-chart will also give some pointers on this, though again take care not to tie the list too tightly to anything that's likely to change.

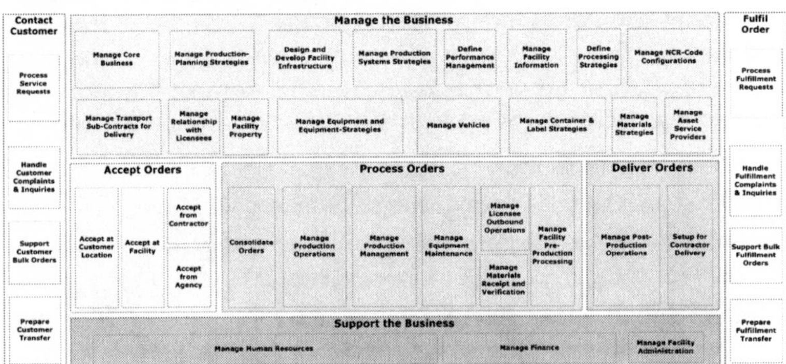

Functions: tier-2 example

Every business function will use assets; take place in locations; be linked by events; and be impacted by laws, rules, regulations, standards, constraints and other business reasons or decisions. So these in turn form a useful set of cross-checks for each function:

- What *assets* does the function use, create change, update, delete, destroy? What category of asset, or combination of asset-categories, is involved in each case – physical, virtual, relational, aspirational, abstract? In what way does the function change the respective asset? In that sense, what category of function, or combination of function-categories, is involved in each case – physical, virtual, relational, aspirational or abstract?

- What *locations* are related to the function? What category of location, or combination of location-categories, is involved in each case - physical, virtual, relational, aspirational, abstract?
- What *events* trigger or are triggered by the function? What category of event, or combination of event-categories, is involved in each case - physical, virtual, relational, aspirational, abstract?
- What *reasons* or decisions apply to or impact on the function? What category of reason, or combination of reason-categories, is involved in each case - rule-based, analytic, heuristic guideline, or principle?

> There's more detail on this, and on how to tackle the other two tiers, in the 'Practice – Services and Functions' chapter in the companion volume *The Service Oriented Enterprise*.
>
> And there's also a matching Visio stencil and template for building a Function Model at tetradianbooks.com/2009/01/services-model/ .

Again, keep it simple - at this stage this is only a first pass, not a full detailed assessment. Gather whatever level of information seems useful, and document it as links between entities in the architecture repository.

Capabilities

Functions need to be linked to capabilities in order to deliver services. A function describes a required change, but on its own has no way to enact that change; and on its own a capability has no function - literally so. Yet we do need to assess each separately, because different combinations of capability and function deliver different services.

> The specification for the Archimate architecture-notation standard includes a useful illustration of this in its insurance-industry example.
>
> - At the higher level, the client sees a single insurance-claims service, implemented in several different ways – different detail-combinations of function and capability, but with the same *overall* business-function – such as a web-interface, a call-centre, a retail storefront, a personal visit by a claims-adjuster, and so on.
> - At the back-office, there are two different services with, again, similar business-functions: one handles claims for below $1000, the other function manages any larger claim. The capabilities used to implement each would be different, because different competencies apply: the lower-value claims can be handled via a rule-based approach, implemented by IT, or by a trainee, perhaps; the higher-value claims require higher levels of skills and

> experience, hence probably a human process perhaps backed up by an IT-based decision-support system.
>
> Same overall function, same overall business service, but with different business-rules, different asset-types, different events or even different locations, will often imply a different combination of capabilities.

This points to the last of the framework columns, and the last of the content that we need to populate in this first pass. To do this, we need to note that whilst Zachman describes capability as 'who', it'd be more accurate to describe it as the real 'how' - the competencies, rather than the activities - of a business-service.

We've left this till last because it's often the most difficult of the lot. The reason is that capabilities inherently merge within themselves *two* sets of categories:

- the set used mainly for *assets*, but also for *functions*, *locations* and *events*: physical, virtual, relational, aspirational, abstract
- the set used mainly for *reasons* and decisions: rule-based, analytic, heuristic, principle-based

The former set indicate how and to what the capability is applied; the latter set represent the required skill-levels:

- *rule-based*: no real skill required, can be implemented via training, or built-in within software or machine function
- *analytic*: requires analytic competence and usually some practical experience; may be built into software, but at significant cost
- *heuristic*: requires genuine skill and practical experience for context-specific interpretation; autonomous software systems possibly but at high cost and high complexity; IT is usually more effective in a decision-support rather than decision-making role
- *principle-based*: requires high degree of skill and ability to cope with inherent uncertainty; not yet feasible to build any IT-based system with this type of capability

As mentioned earlier, there is some natural alignment between these two sets of categories, but not enough that they could fully substitute for each other. So in effect we need to map capabilities using a matrix between the two sets: a clerk might do only simple rule-based decisions on virtual data, which could well be handled better by a software-driven process, but a maintenance engineer or machinist might require a high degree of skill with physical objects, for example, and be very hard to replace by IT alone.

A moment's calculation would show that there are at least twenty cells in that matrix: too many to make it worthwhile to list all the possible assessment-questions here. So for this column, adapt and combine the previous questions on assets, locations and events – see p.43 – with an assessment of skill-levels as above, to arrive at appropriate questions for each cell.

The skill-level assessments will also indicate which capabilities can be implemented by IT, with relative ease, or more expensively, or only with inordinate difficulty, or not at all. With luck, this should dissuade all but the most insanely over-enthusiastic IT-advocates from attempting to build 'solutions' in contexts for which by definition they cannot feasibly work – which should help to defuse some of the anger and angst so often locked up in the bitter relationship between business and IT!

From this, build a capability-map for the enterprise:

- What capabilities are implied as required by the Results Logic Diagram? How would you categorise each capability, in terms of asset-type acted upon and required skill-level?
- What capabilities are implied as required by the Function Model? How would you categorise each capability, in terms of asset-type acted upon and required skill-level?
- What capabilities are implied by each key asset-type, location and event identified in the previous assessments here? What is the required skill-level in each case?
- What capabilities are implied by each key reason, decision, constraint, standard or suchlike identified in the previous assessments here? What is the required skill-level for appropriate decision-making in each case? What asset-types would be involved in each case? What events or functions would call for this capability?
- Does the capability need to vary in different locations? If so, what location-category is implied in each case?

Document the results of these assessments in the upper rows of the 'capability' column in the framework, together with any cross-links as required.

This then completes the population of the base 'holograph' in the framework - the pre-built architecture that we'll need in place before we can do any work under proper architecture governance. The final actions for this step are to define all the governance processes and artefacts that we'll need for subsequent architecture cycles, and the methods, tools and techniques by which we will share and communicate the results of that work.

Architecture governance

The *purpose* of this section is to set up the formal governance processes for the enterprise-architecture capability.

> I've placed this part at the end of this step, rather than at the beginning, because up till this point there won't have been that much need for *architecture* governance – the work will have been done under normal *project* governance instead. But once we've proven the value of the notion of architecture – which we should have done by now, especially with the Function Model – we'll have to tackle the need for governance of the architecture itself, in its own terms.
>
> When you revisit this stage – which you should do on a regular basis, probably at least once or twice a year – you would of course already have all of the governance documents in place. For a revisit, it's probably best to review them *first*, before doing any of the other work of this stage. But for the first pass, we won't need to do it until here.

Note that, from the business perspective, part of that governance is formed by the processes through which you engage others in the architecture 'conversation'.

On the *people* side, this is where we move out from desk-based business-analysis and start to engage with people in general. The range of people you'll need to work with will depend on the chosen scope - a smaller pilot, at the start, but eventually out to the entire enterprise - but people-skills in general will begin to come much more to the fore here, rather than the analytic skills that have been the main requirement so far.

For *planning*, you'll need some kind of 'communication plan' as to how you will engage with the various stakeholders, and a formal process or checklist for defining the required governance.

The *practice* would be based on that communication plan, and the 'governance for governance' process.

> If you're familiar with TOGAF, much of what happens here is a simplified version of TOGAF's Preliminary Phase, combined with the parts of its Phase A 'Architecture Vision' that deal with overall setup for architecture rather than the details for a single iteration.
>
> One important difference is around scope. TOGAF assumes that enterprise architecture will always be a major effort, encompassing the entire enterprise – or all of its IT, anyway. But that isn't what happens in practice: if nothing else, you won't get the funding until you've proven the business value. Instead, pick a small area of the business as a pilot, and do your initial governance-planning and the like for that area alone. Once you've proven the value of the work, you'll need to expand the scope – but at the start, keep it simple, and keep it small.

And whilst ***performance*** would again be measured in project-completion terms, as specified by the project sponsor, perhaps a more important metric would be the indications of acceptance and take-up of the architecture by the broader business community - of which the Function Model would probably be the first example.

Creating engagement

For architecture to be useful, people have to be willing to *use* it. And they'll only be able to use it if they know it exists - which is why it's essential for architects to communicate what they do. Hence the importance of a 'communications plan' and the like - and from there, of tools such as wikis and intranet websites to put that plan into practice.

> Chapter 36 'Architecture Deliverables' in the TOGAF 9 specification includes an all-too-brief description of the role and content of an architecture Communications Plan. As that summary states, mapping out the stakeholders and their communication needs is something we must do right at the start, in Phase A of the cycle – but we then need to *use* that plan, and keep the dialogue going beyond the nominal scope of any single architecture cycle.
>
> The plan is only the start-point of engagement – and that engagement *matters*. Make it happen!

Communication and engagement is the other side of the architect role. The catch is that it's mostly about *people,* not abstract analysis - and that demands a completely different skillset from that we've used so far. For many enterprise architects, dealing with all of the interpersonal politics and other 'people-stuff' is *hard* - but all of our previous work will be in vain unless we *do* tackle it. All those analyses and models and the like may be the backbone of the work, but the real architecture - the place where the architecture is literally 'real-ised' - is always through people. The dialogue *is* the architecture.

> By the way, it's wise here to *expect* that people will tell you "you've got it all wrong", or worse, with disparaging comments about your competence – or lack of it – thrown in for good measure. Painful though it may be, it's a natural consequence of the processes by which people learn in a collective space: meaning *emerges* from a collective conversation about the 'unknown', "I don't know what I want, but I'll know it when I see it". Hence we need something – almost anything, really – to initiate and guide that conversation. Which means that at the start of the conversation, the usual response is "I don't know what I want, but I know that isn't it" – or, in short, "you're wrong".

So don't worry about it, and above all don't over-defend your work: *the architecture is the dialogue*, not just the end-result. Ask their advice, ask what you could do better. That's how engagement happens: and when others become passionate about the architecture, 'owning' what they've co-created with you, you'll know you've succeeded.

Yes, it can be intensely frustrating – insanely, hair-tearingly, mind-bendingly frustrating – when other people 'just don't get it' in relation to the architecture. But that's *our* problem, not theirs: if we want others to 'get it', it's up to *us* to provide conditions under which they *can* 'get it', where they *can* see the benefits of working with others in the enterprise in an architectural way. Some typical reasons why they don't 'get it' would include:

- "this architecture stuff doesn't make sense" – so *we* need to find ways in which it does make sense for them
- "it doesn't apply to our context" – so *we* need to show where it applies, and why
- "it's just theory" – so *we* need to show how it works in practice
- "no-one bothered to ask us" – so *we* need to show where it *does* take their experience into account
- "it's working now, why do have to change it?" – so *we* need to justify, in their terms, the requirements behind the change
- "we don't have time for this stuff!" – so *we* need to show why they don't have time to *not* do 'this stuff'
- "why should we bother to help anyone else?" – so *we* need to show why it's in their own interest to do so

We can't make the architecture happen on our own: an enterprise is about *shared* goals, *shared* vision. So we need to understand that whilst we may have nominal responsibility for the architecture, we don't *possess* it: it belongs to everyone in the enterprise. The architecture will only happen when people feel that they 'own' it too: not imposed on them from above, but something in which they themselves are co-authors, co-creators. That's what engagement is about; that's what it's *for*.

This is one of the reasons why the Function Model is so important: it describes the enterprise in a way that includes *everyone*. Another reason is that it provides a basis for *story* – a story of the enterprise as a whole, as an ecosystem. Each business-process is the thread of a story; each use-case and transaction is a story; with the Function Model we can show how these stories literally weave their way across the organisation and the enterprise, touching different business functions and services and capabilities, using the enterprise assets in different ways and in different locations, triggering other business events for different business reasons. The architecture *is* a story: so to help others make sense of the architecture, tell it *as* a story - a narrative which includes them *in* the story.

> Storytelling is a skill in itself, and one whose business applications and business value are only now beginning to be better understood. One resource we've found useful for this, and for practices on 'narrative knowledge' in general, is the Australian consultancy Anecdote: see their website at www.anecdote.com.au .

Typical techniques for engagement include:

- publishing models and other artefacts - typically via the architecture-toolset
- running your own intranet-website, including wikis and other facilities for feedback - again, some architecture-toolsets will support this requirement 'out of the box'
- seminars and 'public' presentations across the enterprise
- workshops for engagement with operations staff, particularly those with direct involvement in front-line business processes
- maintaining a 'watching-brief' relationship with senior staff, strategists, project-managers and others involved in change-management
- building working-relationships with those responsible for other 'pervasive' themes such as security, privacy, quality, health and safety, ethics and environment

It's unlikely that you would use each of these approaches in a first pass of the architecture, but it's worthwhile considering all of the options from the start, as you'll certainly need them later on.

> In the 'Completions – Closing the loop' chapter in the companion volume *Bridging the Silos* there's more detail on tactics for linking with knowledge-management, change-management, quality-management, communities of practice and other probable allies within the enterprise to help us with these aspects of engagement.

Architecture is a *dialogue*, not a monologue: so perhaps most of all, listening is more important than talking. People are likely to listen to what we have to say only if they feel they too have been heard.

From this, two-way communication creates engagement with people; and engagement in turn creates governance. More precisely, it creates the kind of governance in which people *want* to be involved, because the work has meaning to them. And that's what we're aiming for here: enterprise architecture only becomes the architecture *of* the enterprise when the enterprise in general is engaged in every aspect of its creation and use.

Creating the architecture capability

For the architecture development so far, we've run it as a stand-alone project, or embedded as part of another project. We've reached the first maturity-level, and we've presented the results, as a kind of proto-architecture. Everyone - we hope! - is happy with what we've done: we've proven that architecture is indeed of value to the enterprise.

But that's it: we're done. We can't do it this way again: it works well enough for a first-pass, but it's not sustainable - especially in terms of its governance. To take it further, we need to set it up as a proper enterprise capability, with proper governance and so on.

> What follows will be sufficient to set you up for the next step in architecture maturity, but it doesn't stop there, of course. Each time you change the formal scope of your architecture, or get ready to move up to another maturity-level, you'll need to revisit this work, to review and update the architecture capability and its governance.

Depending on where and at what level you want to move on to next, there can be quite a bit of work to do at this point - almost a mini-project in its own right, in fact. But whilst there's fair bit to do - including a sizeable amount of paperwork, no doubt - it's all straightforward, and for the most part already documented in the TOGAF specification and other architecture descriptions: you'll need to tailor it to your own context, but that's about all that's required. We can summarise it as follows:

- you'll need sufficient *funding*, equipment, work-space and other *resources*
- you'll need the right *people*
- you'll need an appropriate *toolset* and repositories and registers in which to record and maintain that 'body of knowledge about enterprise structure and purpose'
- you'll need formal *governance*, including formal *authority* to engage others in the work
- you'll need to define *governance-artefacts* to be created, updated and used within the architecture cycle itself

It's not really feasible here to describe how to obtain the right ***funding*** and ***resources***: that'll depend on the nature of the organisation, its organisational culture and structure, on the scope to be covered by the architecture capability, and a whole host of other context-specific factors. All we can say for certain here is that it'll have to be done, and probably done first. But having done all the previous work of this step, you should now be able to *prove* the potential business-value of architecture - which means it should be a lot easier than trying to argue the business-case from scratch.

Finding the right *people* and bringing them on board will, again, be somewhat context-dependent. But by now - such as from the comments earlier, under 'People - governance' in *Preparing for architecture* (p.10) - you'll have a better idea of the range of skill-sets that'll be needed for the next stage: so again this should be easier than starting to build the right team from scratch.

> Chapter 52 'Architecture Skills Framework' in the TOGAF9 specification summarises the skillsets needed for IT-architecture. It doesn't extend much beyond that scope, but it does at least suggest the probable skills and levels of experience needed at each maturity-level for true whole-of-enterprise architecture. Recommended.

The same applies to ***toolsets*** and repositories: we explored those issues under 'Planning - frameworks' in *Preparing for architecture* (p.18). You should review those facilities and capabilities there as part of this activity - for example, you'll soon be needing a purpose-built architecture toolset if you're not already using one, and you'll need to include a dispensations-register as part of the repositories for all further architecture work. But it's all straight-forward enough: it just needs to be done - and paid for, which may be the hardest part!

The main work here will be around ***governance*** - in particular, developing and documenting all the requisite procedures - and ***governance-artefacts*** used within the architecture-cycle.

> In the companion volume *Bridging the Silos*, the chapter 'Completion – Architecture-artefacts' provides summaries of the purpose and content for most of the documents used in the modified Architecture Development Method described here (see p.20). In the lists below, documents described or referenced in *Bridging the Silos* are shown with a number-sign (#).
>
> There's also a whole section in the TOGAF 9 specification – the Architecture Capability Framework – that deals with governance and related documents, whilst its Chapter 36, 'Architecture Deliverables', provides brief summaries of the purpose and content of a whole range of typical architecture-artefacts. These are fairly comprehensive, but unfortunately many of the descriptions are scrambled by TOGAF's obsessive IT-centrism – for example, its insistence that architecture-governance is a subset of IT-governance – so we need to do a certain

amount of translation before we can use them in real whole-of-enterprise architecture. (The specification is further scrambled in that it also includes descriptions of several documents that relate to *implementation*-governance rather than *architecture*-governance – which don't belong there at all.) In the lists below, documents described or referenced in the TOGAF specification are marked with an asterisk (*).

Typical governance-procedures and related documents for overall architecture governance include:

- *Architecture Governance* # * and *Architecture Board* * – defines the governance processes for the architecture itself
- *Architecture Charter* # * – identifies and defines the formal authority and responsibilities for architecture as a business capability or business unit
- *Architecture Principles* # * – identifies and describes the principles used to govern architectural decisions, with applicable higher-level principles included by reference
- *Architecture Standards* # * – identifies and describes the formal and other standards used to guide architecture decisions and designs, with external standards usually included by reference

Formal governance procedures and work-instructions will also be needed for management of the architecture-repository, requirements repository, risks and opportunities register, issues register, dispensations register and glossary and thesaurus. Since it's likely, though, that these will also be shared outside of architecture, their governance will probably need to be beyond the authority of architecture itself.

Typical architecture-cycle governance-artefacts include:

- *Request for Architecture Work* # * – describes the business-questions and context to be addressed in an architecture-cycle
- *Statement of Architecture Work* # * – maintains a record of all architecture work and decisions in the current architecture-cycle
- *Architecture Roadmap* * – overview of proposed changes arising from a large-scale architecture-assessment in 'classic' enterprise-architecture
- *Project-plan* or *Migration-plan* # * – overview and/or detailed description of a proposed project or portfolio of projects
- *Architecture Compliance Statement* # * and associated checklists * (for IT only) – asserts the extent to which a proposed

implementation complies with the specified architecture, and describes reasons for any non-compliance

- *Architecture Description Statement #* – simplified Architecture Compliance Statement used in 'hands-off' architecture (see p.167)
- *Architecture Position Statement #* – describes architect's recommended response to non-compliance in an Architecture Compliance Statement or Architecture Description Statement
- *Architecture Dispensation Statement #* – describes architect's reasons for permitting a non-compliant implementation, and recommendations for future review and resolution
- *Phase-completion reports #* – describes the activities and results of an architecture-cycle Phase, and includes stakeholder sign-off for the respective Phase

Governance will also be needed to manage some other concerns such as security and visibility of architecture models, descriptions, frameworks, roadmaps definitions and other products from the architecture work.

You may need other governance processes and artefacts in your own specific context, but these at least should serve as a start.

Resources

- TOGAF (The Open Group Architecture Framework): see www.opengroup.org/architecture/togaf9-doc/arch/
- Adapting TOGAF for whole-of-enterprise scope: see Tom Graves, *Bridging the Silos: enterprise architecture for IT-architects* (Tetradian, 2008)
- Business Motivation Model: see businessrulesgroup.org/bmm.shtml
- Vision, role, mission, goal: see Tom Graves, *Real Enterprise Architecture: beyond IT to the whole enterprise* (Tetradian, 2008)
- Visioning and purpose in service-oriented architecture: see Tom Graves, *The Service Oriented Enterprise: enterprise architecture and viable services* (Tetradian, 2009)
- SEMPER diagnostic and metric: see Tom Graves, *SEMPER and SCORE: enhancing enterprise effectiveness* (Tetradian, 2008)
- Online version of SEMPER diagnostic: see www.sempermetrics.com
- ITIL (IT Infrastructure Library) and primacy of services: see www.itil-officialsite.com

📖 Archimate specification: see *Archimate Practically* (Archimate Foundation, 2007) and www.archimate.org

🕸 Business storytelling and narrative knowledge: see www.anecdote.com.au

STEP 2: CLEAN UP THE MESS

By this stage we've now verified that our architecture has a fair notion of what the business is, and what 'value' *means* within the overall enterprise. We also have a reasonable overview of the assets, functions, locations, capabilities and events important in the enterprise, and the drivers that impact on the business. In short, we have the key content for the framework 'holograph'.

Which means we have enough to start building a *usable* enterprise architecture, adding identifiable business value at every step. And the first task is to tidy up the structural mess that will have accumulated over the years - because if we don't do this, anything we build on top will just make things worse.

We start small, with small, localised projects that each tackle some clearly-defined issue - usually rationalising a duplication of effort, or creating simple improvements in cross-functional efficiency. Through these, we build up our experience and credibility until we're ready to tackle 'the big one': the typical Gordian knot of a tangle in which everything depends on everything else.

> This is traditional TOGAF territory – the classic 'big bang' 'architecting the enterprise', or at least re-architecting its IT. But note what we've done before we get here: we *don't* do it as our first activity, as the TOGAF specification suggests that we should. Instead, we'll have built up sufficient 'street-cred' such that it'll be *obvious* to almost everyone that this is the next thing we need to do. Which means that it'll be a lot less of a fight to get the necessary funding, resources, stakeholder cooperation and so on.
>
> More to the point, if we don't do it this way, with a quiet build-up in the background, a fight is what we'll face, because no-one would believe we can deliver the purported business value. This way, we'll have already *proved* we can deliver business value. Credibility *matters*.

If in doubt, there's a simple way to test whatever we intend to do:

Every architecture activity begins with an explicit business reason – for explicit business value.

So throughout this step, quietly, steadily, we extend the capability from 'ad-hoc' fixes, to structures that *demonstrably* deliver results that are more efficient, reliable and repeatable.

Purpose and strategy: The focus here is on efficiency and cost-management, primarily through '***horizontal***' rationalisation and optimisation of the enterprise's systems - in the broadest sense of 'system'.

> Again, much of this is familiar TOGAF territory – classic IT-architecture and the like. The main difference is that we'll often include other aspects of the enterprise – we don't assume that the world begins and ends with IT – and we'll usually do the 'to-be' first, *before* the 'as-is', to minimise the amount we're constrained by assumptions about existing systems.

People and governance: At the start, we'll continue with much the same small team of generalists, using the governance-cycle outlined for the extended-TOGAF described earlier (see p.20). As time goes on, though, we're likely to need to co-opt quite a few other domain-architects into the team, and most of those will need IT-specific skillsets, because many of the problems we're likely to meet here will be in the IT domains.

> This does *not* mean, though, that we treat architecture governance as a subset of IT-governance, as TOGAF suggests. The two separate streams of governance need to come together in the architecture – which means you'll have at least two sets of stakeholders you'll need to manage, each with their own very different perspectives, priorities and opinions. As the architect, it's *your* responsibility to somehow get these often warring tribes to reach agreement on each architectural issue... oh joys... Welcome to the *real* world of enterprise-architecture!

Planning and frameworks: The core item you'll need for this is the Function Model - which is why it was so important to set it up during the previous step. You'll also need to end up with a set of reference-frameworks, describing the bindedness of specific components and requirements across the IT-domains and elsewhere; and probably also a set of 'blueprints' for change. You won't have these available on the first-pass through this step, of course, but you'll need to review them here in each subsequent pass.

> Another oft-quoted resource in this context is Ross, Weill and Robertson's book *Enterprise Architecture as Strategy*. It's mostly about enterprise IT-architecture rather than the broader sense of 'enterprise-architecture' that we're using here, but there's enough emphasis on business and the overall 'operating model' such that, with a bit of care and sideways-thinking, its ideas, principles and practices can be extended beyond the IT domain. Recommended, anyway.

Practice and methods: For each section of work, use the standard TOGAF ADM architecture-cycle, or, better, the extended-ADM cycle described earlier (see p.20), because it's designed specifically for the kind of iterative Agile-style architecture we'll need here.

Again, you'll find more detail on the extended TOGAF cycle in the 'Methodology' chapters of the companion volume *Bridging the Silos: enterprise architecture for IT-architects* – see the *Resources* section at the end of the chapter.

Performance, end-products and metrics: There's a lot of work in this section, and to do it properly is going to take several months at least: it's important to manage expectations, and make sure that no-one is under any illusions about that timescale. What you *can* do to ease the pain is split it up into smaller chunks, each aligned to specific business needs and deliverables, as described earlier in the chapter. At some point, you *will* have to tackle 'the big one', the real 'spaghetti factory' of tangled IT-interdependencies that the TOGAF methods are mainly designed to address: but before that, it's best to get some practice in on smaller, safer projects!

Typical artefacts from this step would include:

- standard architecture-models: business-systems, information-systems, application- and data-architectures; also technology-infrastructure overviews (though detailed models would usually be left until a later pass)
- preliminary TOGAF-style 'change-roadmap' or equivalents
- reports, architecture-scenario models, requirements and other outcomes of 'architecture-adviser' engagement in projects

Whichever way you do it, always ensure that the expected business-value for each piece of work is outlined *beforehand*, and preferably in explicit, measurable terms such as cost-savings or identifiable improvements in overall effectiveness. If you do that, you'll be able to *prove* the business worth of the work - which is something you really *must* establish here. It's true that you'll be adding a lot of useful information to the architecture repositories and so on as you go: but most people won't be able to see the value of that until much further down to the track. For now, you *must* measure your value mostly in terms that have immediate meaning for the business.

Business-systems and information-systems

The ***purpose*** of this section is to identify and describe the core decisions for the ideal 'to-be' of the overall structure of support for the business - particularly its information systems. This provides an agreed base for all future decisions.

For *people*, you'll need the usual business-analysis skillsets, with an emphasis on information architecture (hence including but broader than detail-level IT-architecture and data-architecture).

For *planning*, the models to be developed will all draw from the Function Model. You'll also need general overviews and perhaps some detail-descriptions of your existing information-systems.

> To do the work in this section, the Function Model needs to be complete and approved to tier-3 at least, and preferably some tier-4 tasks also listed, to clarify information-usage and -boundaries. If the model isn't yet at that level, the first part of this work will be to extend it accordingly – see p.49 to review how to do this.
>
> Tier-3 activities are clusters of related tasks that typically represent the main focus of a single person's work. Aim to include perhaps 250-300 of these overall in the model, contained within their tier-2 clusters.
>
> Note that almost everyone will want you to list *all* of their activities on the Function Model! Instead, work with them to summarise down to perhaps half a dozen tier-3 activities per tier-2 cluster, and record all the other details as tier-4 tasks.

The *practice* should follow the standard architecture-cycle, with an emphasis on 'to-be', with minimal need for implementation governance.

For *performance*, the key business outcome is improved communication, especially between business and IT, and clarity on future strategy overall. Wherever practicable, identify any demonstrable cost-savings arising from that improved communication. The main artefacts will be the Business Systems and Information Systems models.

> There's a huge business-benefit to be gained here, but typically it's not in the form of immediate cost-savings: you'll perhaps need to make that point clear to your sponsors. (Those cost-savings do start coming through a little later, though, starting with the next section – but to get there we do need to do this work first.)
>
> The real measure of success here is in improved communication, improved pre-agreement, reduced duplication of effort and reduced amounts of 'running off on the wrong track'. The costs-savings there can be enormous – but they *are* indirect, not direct. Make certain that that point is fully understood before you start!

Business systems

Modelling the enterprise in terms of its business functions - in the Function Model - provides a base on which to build a variety of valuable overlays for the architecture of the enterprise. The first of these is the Business Systems Model.

The aim here is to identify groups of activities that perform the same kinds of functions and share similar kinds of information, and hence should be supported by similar information-systems, even though their operational processes may be different. This should help us to ensure that any systems developed or purchased to manage this information don't overlap in function or in the information that they store.

> Remember that the scope for enterprise-architecture is wider than IT alone. Much of the core information of an enterprise is word-of-mouth, or in individual or collective memory, or built into work-instructions for machines and the like: IT plays an important part, but it's by no means the only part. So look at 'information systems' in the broadest, most generic terms – not solely the information that's in computer networks and databases.

The simplest way to do this is by using colour-coding for the tier-3 activities on the Function Model. Each colour-code represents a different 'business system', or clustering of related activities. For example, we could split some of the business-systems by service-category-type:

- Is the information about developing the business, changing the business, or routine management of the business?
- Is it about a specific value-chain or type of delivery-service?
- Is it about funding, or people-management, or customer-relationships?

And so on, and so on. The most appropriate split will depend on the nature of the enterprise, so there are no standard guidelines, but aim to identify some ten to twenty distinct shared areas of information.

Identifying business-systems

- Which tier-3 activities, whether in the same part or different parts of the enterprise, have similar functions and share much the same information?
- What IT-systems or other information-systems should these activities use? In IT terms, what applications are or should be used to store and access this information?
- As a cross-check, what existing business-information, information-systems, applications or business-processes do *not* seem to be used by any activity on the Function Model? What changes would this suggest to the Function Model itself?

Note that you may also need to rethink the levelling or structure of the Function Model somewhat if you can't assign an activity to a business-system, or if you seem to be forced to split an activity between two or more business-systems. That may also be a reason to rethink your business-system boundaries – which would also be the case if you end up with a business-system that seems to have only one or two members.

At the end of this process, you should have a colour-coded version of the Function Model diagram, in which every tier-3 activity has been assigned to just *one* business-system.

From this, make up a set of detailed diagrams, one for each of the business systems, together with an appropriate text-description. There's no standard layout for the individual-system diagrams, but a typical approach is to place the respective tier-3 activities in the middle, with connections between each other, and to other business-systems and external actors shown on the outer edges.

Modelling individual business-systems

Activities are *functions*: something happens, something is changed. Each function uses *assets* of different types – physical, virtual (e.g. data, messages, event-signals), relational (e.g. customer relationships), abstract (e.g. finance). For the Information System Model which follows after this, we need to focus on data-flows, but in the Business System model it's important to also take note of flows of other asset-types.

For each tier-3 activity in this business-system:

- What – if anything – is passed between this activity and each of the other activities in this business-system? What *asset-types* are involved in this transfer? If possible, simplify or summarise each connection between activities to a *single* description, as a single one-way or two-way flow of one or more asset-types.
- What – if anything – is passed between this activity and any of the other Business Systems? What asset-types are involved in this transfer? If possible, simplify or summarise each connection between the activity and Business System to a *single* description, as a single flow of one or more asset-types.
- What is passed between this activity and other actors outside of the scope of the Function Model? What asset-types are involved in this transfer? If possible, simplify or summarise

each connection between activity and external actor to a *single* description, as a single flow of one or more asset-types.

Add symbols for other Business Systems and for other outside actors to the diagram only if they are referenced by activities within this Business System.

> In our models, we used the following conventions:
>
> - *Activity*: rounded-corner rectangle, with an icon in one corner to indicate manual, IT-based, machine-based or composite process.
> - *Other Business System*: rectangle coloured as per the main Business Systems index-model.
> - *External actor*: circle.
> - Data or message (*virtual*) link: narrow solid line.
> - Flows of *physical* objects: narrow dashed line.
> - Customer-contacts and other *relational* links: narrow dotted line.
> - Other asset-types or composite links: broader double-line.
>
> We assigned to each flow a brief descriptive label that summarised both the content and purpose of the flow.

Information systems and 'single source of truth'

For each business system, we should now have a summary of the information flows between activities. To identify all the information systems, we also need to assess information used *within* each activity. So to complete this set of models, we need to review the business activities to verify the 'chunks' of IT-type systems and other information-related functions and the like that would be required to support those business activities. We then summarise these chunks of functionality and related storage as abstract 'information systems'. They're 'logical' in that they don't describe any specific IT application, for example, but do describe in broad terms what IT and other applications should do.

> We define the information systems at the whole-of-enterprise level, and *without reference to existing IT applications*. Strictly speaking, it's not even a 'to-be' – a picture of what actual systems we would have at a particular future time – but more an *idealised* view of what ought to exist to support the needs in a perfect world. This ensures that, overall, the activities and information systems each perform functions that make sense to perform together; that there are no overlaps in functionality; and that all of the required functionality is covered.

The resultant Information Systems Model consists of an overview diagram or 'context diagram' and a set of more detailed diagrams for each of the 'information systems', together with a textual explanation of the content and role of each system.

At the end of this process, each business-system should be aligned with just *one* matching information-system. There would usually be a variety of applications that might draw on and manipulate that information, but preferably a *single* shared data-store in each case. That's certainly the ideal for any 'to-be' design, though it may not work out that way in practice - especially not in the 'as-is' setup. But what we're really aiming for here is that for each business-system, there is just one 'database of record': a *single source of truth*, in the information sense of the term.

> In our Information Systems models, we used much the same conventions as for the individual Business Systems. The only addition was that the information source was shown by a 'cylinder' symbol – the symbol for a database in many standard IT diagram-types.
>
> For Information Systems which are not centred on IT – for example, those in which information is transferred mainly by word-of-mouth, or knowledge stored in personal experience – it's still important to record that fact: in such cases, perhaps use a dotted or dashed line in the 'database' symbol, for relational or physical memory respectively.

Identifying single-source-of-truth

For each identified business-system and its information-system:

- What are the sources for transaction-data, information and knowledge for this system?
- Who or what may create, read, update or delete transaction-records for this system? For what purposes?
- Who or what may collate transaction-records into aggregations or transformations such as counts-of, trends-of, averages-of and suchlike? For what purposes? Via what transform-processes? Where and in what systems are such transforms maintained? Who or what may create, read, update or delete these transforms, or the means by which the transforms take place?
- What audit-trails exist for changes and aggregations of data, information and knowledge for this system?
- What services does each information-item provide or support?
- Is there a 'single source of truth' for information in this system? If not, what are the consequences of having more than one source of truth?

Reassess the information-systems, the business-systems, and all the way back to the Function Model, in the light of the results of this review.

Later on, when you revisit this work in a future review, you'll also need to model equivalent systems that support the physical flows, the people-relationships and so on, to make up a description for all asset-types – in fact you may need to do some of those straight away if you're in a logistics business, say, or in a recruitment or sales-oriented context. The main reason we usually do the information-systems first is because they're so often the source of so much immediate business pain...

Do those other assessments in much the same way as for the information-systems: adapt the questions above to suit, and create the models accordingly.

What do we have?

The *purpose* of this section is to gain a better understanding of the 'as-is' condition of the architecture, and make a start on cleaning up the mess.

Let's be blunt about this: you're about to discover, painfully, that your systems are in one heck of a mess. But don't panic: *everyone* faces this mess as soon as they get going on the real enterprise architecture.

Every medium-sized company that's been around for a decade or two and has gone through a few merger / acquisition cycles will have a tangled web of legacy-systems, a proliferation of small point-solutions that were supposed to be temporary fixes but have somehow become permanent, and a whole bunch of pointless processes and reports that no-one reads. Yes, it's inefficient, ineffective, a real waste of effort, and embarrassing,, too; but it's what will always happen if there's no architecture to keep it clean – and everyone's system is like this at the start of architecture development. The point is that if you don't clean up the mess, anything you add will only make the mess worse: and the first task in cleaning it up is to be honest about its existence.

Might be a good idea to warn your sponsors beforehand, though: it'll be nasty, but probably best if it's not a nasty surprise as well!

On the *people* side, it's business-analysis again - though probably with even more of an emphasis on IT, because that's where the worst of the mess most often accumulates. You'll be collecting and cataloguing a lot of information here, so in a larger organisation it may also be useful to co-opt some skilled clerical support.

To do this work well, you'll need the right and the authority to ask awkward questions and go prying into any dark corners – so make sure you have that authority behind you before you start, and that everyone knows it, too, or all the ensuing arguments will really slow you down.

Expect people to be a bit defensive, and protective of their own private point-solutions. Make it clear that no-one's questioning the *need* for

> what the point-solution does: all we're doing at first here is building a catalogue of what people have and what each system does. and only later – and *with* their involvement – will we start to do the clean-up.

For ***planning***, what you'll mainly do here is build catalogues and, later, rationalise to reduce redundancies and duplications and seek out synergies, working towards that desired 'single source of truth'. In most cases it's not worth building many models and diagrams of the 'as-is', though you'll certainly need to do so for the various 'to-be' scenarios.

> Again, let's be blunt about it: this clean-up is going to take a long time. In a large organisation, the cataloguing alone will take many months; the full clean-up and rationalisation may well take years. *Much* longer than the business will be willing to pay for up-front – which is why things got into this mess in the first place, in fact. But there's no getting round it: it *is* a lot of effort, and it *does* all have to be done before any real cost-savings start rolling in.
>
> The trick is to split it into smaller, more manageable chunks – more palatable in cost-terms, too. And the natural 'chunk'-boundaries are the Business Systems and Information Systems – which is why you need to do that part of the work first.
>
> Working with your sponsors, pick out a priority-sequence for the Business Systems, and work your way steadily through the list as time and budget permit. If you set up the priorities right, each segment of clean-up will be paid for by the savings from the previous segments, and you'll have demonstrable business-value all the way.

The ***practice*** should follow the full standard architecture-cycle, with an emphasis on 'as-is'. The activities are summarised below under the standard phase-headings.

> A quick reminder that the architecture-cycle we're using here is not the standard TOGAF ADM, but the amended version of the ADM from *Bridging the Silos* – see p.21 above for an explanation of the differences and the reasons behind them.

For ***performance***, the key business outcome is a steady move towards rationalisation of the assets and functionality used in the business and its processes - leading not only to cost-savings, but to clarity, simplicity and improved *effectiveness* overall. The main artefacts here will be system-inventories of any items in scope: typically physical IT systems, software, applications and data-structures on a first pass through the work of this section, but on subsequent passes may - and ultimately should - include any other physical assets or virtual assets, and machine- and/or manual-based 'applications' of direct relevance to the business.

Phase A: define scope for rationalisation

In accordance with the Architecture Charter - see 'Creating the architecture capability', in the later part of the work for Step 1 (p.60) - the list of priorities for the Business Systems and the like is a stack of Request for Architecture Work items, each implying its own architecture cycle. So specifying the scope and activities for this type of architecture cycle should be straightforward: it's already defined by the scope of the respective Business System, Information System or whatever item it is that's the next on the priority stack.

> Note that, exactly as with TOGAF, we *do* eventually cover the whole architecture of the entire enterprise. (In fact we cover a lot more than TOGAF, because we don't restrict ourselves to TOGAF's IT-centric scope.) The difference here is that we *don't* try to do it all at once: we do it piece by piece, one Business System at a time – which makes everything a lot simpler, every step of the way.

Expanding the Request for Architecture Work

For the identified Business System or other work-item:

- What is the scope for assessment, in terms of framework cells (see 'Planning - frameworks' in *Preparing for architecture*, p.13)? What composites and real-world 'things' are represented in this scope?
- Who are the stakeholders for this scope? What authority will you need to work with these stakeholders, to ask questions and to catalogue and suggest redesigns for the respective systems? How will you create and maintain engagement with these stakeholders?
- How, where and in what form will the resultant inventory be created and stored? Who will have access to this information, how, and for what purposes?
- Who will authorise, fund and provide resources for any required redesigns?

Document the answers, actions and authorisations in a Statement of Architecture Work, get it signed off by the stakeholders as per the current governance procedures, and get down to work.

Phase B: inventory the existing items in scope

The 'as-is' activity is also straightforward: it's just an inventory of whatever the enterprise has in that scope. The only complication will be that people are often fiercely protective of 'their' private applications and data and the like - and with good reason, too, because often it's those small point-solutions that provide the cross-functional or cross-layer 'glue' that holds the real business-processes together. In *this* part of the work, all we're doing is finding out what exists at present: use that fact to reassure people, and gain their trust and confidence to get them to show you how their part of the enterprise *really* works.

> Most of the better architecture-toolsets will already have a template for this type of inventory – otherwise make up your own, as a spreadsheet or small database, or preferably in the metamodel of the toolset itself. Either way, aim to end up with a structure that as far as practicable is the same for *every* type of item: that way you'll be able to build reports that can draw from any mix of item-types. Item-identifiers and brief summaries should also end up in the shared Glossary, with any synonyms, homonyms, heteronyms or other naming-conflicts also cross-referenced in the shared Thesaurus.

Develop an 'as-is' inventory of the respective items

For each item in scope, information to inventory would include:

- How is the item *identified*? What names and acronyms are used for it, in what contexts? Do any of these identifiers conflict with those of other items? If so, how are those naming-conflicts resolved?
- What does the item *do*? What roles or functions does it play, in which business-processes? Who are the stakeholders for what the item does?
- What does the item *cost*? In what sense of 'cost'? - money, skills, maintenance-effort, licence-constraints, auditing costs or whatever? How would these costs change through the item's life-cycle?
- What is the item's *status*? For example, is it business-critical and in live use; or provides low-priority reports; or perhaps is just experimental, something with which to test out ideas? Is it one of several parallel uses - development, test, production? Where is it within a typical life-cycle - idea-stage, development, pre-production, commissioning, live, mature, sunset, or probably or actually superseded?
- What cross-dependencies does it have? What other items does it use? What other items use it? Who - if known - are the stakeholders for each of those cross-dependencies?

- Who owns the item? In what sense - with what responsibility - do they own the item? What procedures exist to manage handovers of those responsibilities?

Document the results in the architecture repositories and registers, and get the stakeholders to sign it off as an acceptable description of the 'as-is' for the respective context.

> Do be realistic about this, of course. Despite John Zachman's oft-quoted assertion, we don't *need* every 'excruciating detail' about every possible item – especially for all the myriad of small-yet-important point-solutions. Instead, keep the focus here on gathering *enough* information to make sense of what's going on and what everything does: you don't need to go any deeper than 'just enough' – especially not on a first-pass, where the highest priority is to pick out some 'low-hanging fruit' for quick-wins and quick business-value.
>
> Do keep a watch, though, for any dependencies which cross Business Systems or Information System boundaries. In reality, those boundaries must always be somewhat porous, to bridge across the silos: but if there are too many 'external' cross-dependencies – especially amongst those business-critical yet near-invisible point-solutions – they can break the integrity of the Business System structure. In extreme cases, you may need to go back and rethink that structure from scratch: but do use those cross-dependencies as another validation-test for the structure, anyway.

Phase C: identify the required rationalisation

In principle, the work here should be minimal: everything for the ideal 'to-be' is already documented in the Business System and its associated Information System. In practice, though, the Systems descriptions will almost certainly be over-idealised, and probably too simplistic compared to the finer detail highlighted in assessing all those point-solutions. Avoiding any assumptions about the supposed essentiality of any existing or future items - because we shouldn't look at 'solutions' at all until Phase E - outline an intermediate 'to-be' that seems achievable, in terms of probable time and budget, as a step towards that 'ideal' system-structure.

> The questions here are much the same as in the previous Phase: the only real difference is that the answers will be in future-tense rather than past- or present-tense.
>
> Where practicable, use the same inventory-template to document this: doing so will make the gap-analysis in the next Phase a great deal easier.

Develop a 'to-be' inventory of the respective items

For each item in scope, information to inventory would include:

- How would the item be *identified*? What names and acronyms are used for it, in what contexts? What continuity or clashes would there be with identifiers for any 'as-is' items?
- What would the item *do*? What roles or functions would it play, in which business-processes? Who would the stakeholders be for what the item does?
- What would the item *cost*, and in what sense of 'cost'? How would these costs change through the item's life-cycle?
- What would the item's *status* be? In what sense of 'status'?
- What cross-dependencies would it need to have? What other items would it use, or use it? Who – if known – would the stakeholders be for each of those cross-dependencies?
- Who would own the item? In what sense of 'own'? What procedures would need to exist to manage handovers of those ownership-responsibilities?

As before, document the results in the architecture repositories and registers, and get the stakeholders to sign it off as the 'to-be' for the respective context.

> It's likely that, tucked away amongst the smaller point-solutions identified in the previous Phase, there will be some real 'hidden gems' – particularly for tackling 'pervasive' themes such as quality, privacy and trust. Watch out for those, and include them – or at least, the descriptions of their roles and functionality - in your 'to-be' assessment here.

Phase D: establish gap and change-requirements

Again, this should be straightforward enough: it's a standard TOGAF-style gap-analysis, in fact. Yet note that we can only do it once the work of the previous two Phases is complete: we need to resist any temptation or pressure to rush down here – or, worse, a rush to 'solutions' – before that work is properly finalised and signed-off, because that'd be the only way we'll ensure we have a solid suggestion of the real requirements we need.

Identify requirements, risks and responsibilities

Contrasting items across the whole specified scope, questions to consider would include:

- What is the gap between the current 'as-is' and the desired 'to-be'?
- What should be kept? What should change? What should be added? What should be dropped? And why?

- What other implications and consequences arise from each apparent gap?
- What requirements, responsibilities, risks, opportunities and other issues are indicated from the previous questions?

Document the results as a gap-analysis matrix and prioritised set of change-requirements, together with appropriate entries in the risks, issues and other registers as required. Once complete, get the stakeholders to sign-off the requirements, and authorise the next phase of work on preliminary solution-designs.

Phase E: outline the required rationalisation activities

At this point we now have an agreed set of requirements for the rationalisation of the Business System or whatever: which means that at this point we pass the baton to the solution-architects, the solution-designers, the project-managers and the like.

Solution-architects specify constraints for a family of solutions; solution-designers develop the details of what needs to be done; project-managers determine the details of how and when it's to be done; and so on. But *it's not our responsibility any more*: we have to let it go. That can be surprisingly hard... but our role here must transform to that of a watching-brief, assisting rather than driving the change.

> The previous Phases were structured somewhat differently from the TOGAF ADM, because we need a broader scope than TOGAF's predefined package; but here we come back to something closer to the TOGAF standard. We still need to strip out its irrelevant IT-centrism, and we can skip much of one of the key pieces of TOGAF work here – split the change-everything-at-once into more manageable 'work-packages' – because we've already set up the simpler Business System scope way back in Phase A; but otherwise it works well enough.
>
> Mostly, anyway. The governance rules, roles and responsibilities shift radically as we move away from ideas about architecture, and on to actual organisational change: and the TOGAF 9 specification for this Phase does describe the changed roles and responsibilities here quite well. But unfortunately it all but scrambles its assignments of who does what and when, with the architect at times apparently the ultimate authority for everything, and at other times seemingly with nothing to do at all. Confusing, to say the least...
>
> The best way to read the TOGAF specification here is to remember that the architect is not the sponsor, but an advisor to and *agent* of the sponsor. And it's the sponsor – typically the CIO or CEO – who has the ultimate responsibility for decisions here. Likewise it's the *solution*-architects – not the enterprise-architects – who are responsible for

guiding *solution*-designs: an important distinction, because the requisite mindsets and skillsets are often radically different. And the responsibility for *managing* change rests with the change-authority – the project-, programme- and portfolio-managers. The responsibilities – and, equally important, the authorities – of the enterprise architects reside solely in enterprise-architecture itself: outside of those bounds, we're just another group of stakeholders, just like everyone else.

Guide handover of change-requirements to solution-architects

Architects and others assess options for implementing the requirements identified in the previous Phases. Appropriate questions from enterprise-architects would include:

- How well do the proposed changes align with the *intent* of the rationalisation? For example, are there any aspects of the solution which would fragment a Business System, or bind two or more Business Systems too tightly together? Or equally, do the other stakeholders have suggestions from their own practical experience that could improve the architecture?
- Do the proposals implement the architecture principles all the way through from root to tip of the respective 'value-tree' for each principle? Do the architectural and operational implications of the enterprise vision and values pervade every aspect of the solution-space?
- Are there any architecture-dispensations - previous breaches of architecture-principles that were forced by real-world constraints - that apply to any existing solutions in this scope? If so, is there any opportunity here to review and resolve those dispensations, to prevent a non-optimal solution becoming even further entrenched as 'accepted practice'?

Document the results in accordance with the change-governance rules, and join the stakeholders to sign-off for approval to move to development of detailed project-proposals.

Phase F: assist in detailed rationalisation-project design

In this part of the work, enterprise-architecture will move even further into the background, as the baton passes from solution-architects and programme-managers to the detail-level solution-designers and the project-managers for individual projects. We still maintain an active watching-brief on behalf of the sponsor, but that's almost where our responsibilities end here.

Most of the work around naming, partitioning, function, value-trees and existing dispensations will have already been done in the previous Phase, though there'll still be some practical concerns on coordinating end-to-end flows across Business Systems, and on constraints that might seem to demand new dispensations. But in essence the architecture questions here are the same as in the previous Phase: they just move down a notch or two towards the finer-grained detail.

> One architectural approach that may help a great deal here is the service-oriented view: whatever the level of detail, *everything* in the entire enterprise is or delivers a service.
>
> The concept of 'service-oriented architecture' is fairly well-understood for detail-level IT, but perhaps less so outside of that domain. Another book in this series, *The Service Oriented Enterprise*, describes the application of service-concepts across the whole enterprise: note in particular the practical implications of *coordinating-services* that guide 'horizontal' connections across the enterprise, and *pervasive-services* that anchor every function, asset, decision and so on back to the enterprise principles and values.

Provide architectural guidance during detailed-design

Appropriate questions from enterprise-architects would include:

- How are items within the design identified? What standards are used for naming-schemes and suchlike? How are naming-conflicts resolved, both within and between name-spaces?
- How does each interface and service communicate with others, both within the Business System and, especially, beyond it? What standards are used for messaging, information-flows, physical-object specifications and so on?
- How is each service to be managed? How is the performance of each to be monitored? In what ways would performance-metrics be aggregated to provide meaningful 'big-picture' overviews across the Business System and beyond?
- Are all architecture principles and values – especially key principles such as quality, security, safety and 'safe-fail' for business-continuity – adequately addressed throughout every part of each solution-design?
- Do any existing architecture-dispensations apply in this scope? Are there any real-world constraints that might demand a dispensation?

Document the results in accordance with the change-governance rules, and join the stakeholders to sign-off for approval to move to implementation.

Phase G: assist in implementation of rationalisation

The detailed governance of the implementation process - design, development, test, commission and roll-out - would always be the responsibility of change-management. Yet enterprise-architecture does have two distinct roles here: as 'client' for the overall work of the Business System rationalisation; and as architecture advisor, to ensure that all changes during implementation do support and reinforce the updated architecture.

> TOGAF 9 does give some detailed guidance here, but as in both the previous Phases, the description is somewhat scrambled: as usual, it's too IT-centric, and the assignments of responsibilities often seem to be all but random. It tries so hard to be generic that in the end it fails to provide any solid linkage to any consistent system of governance...
>
> Which can be a bit of a problem, but not an insurmountable one. The way out is to recognise that architecture *only* does architecture, whilst change-management manages change: we don't blur the boundaries between these roles. If you read through the TOGAF 9 specification with that point in mind, it should all make reasonable sense.

Governance-models vary widely, especially at the kind of scope we're dealing with here, in a major rationalisation programme. In a typical framework such as PRINCE2, though, there will be a number of defined 'gateways' at which each project will undergo some kind of review, usually leading to a 'go/no-go' decision about continuing on with the project. Ideally, architecture should be involved at each of these gateways.

Provide architectural guidance during gateway review

Architecture involvement in gateway-reviews typically takes the form of a call-and-response:

- Under change-management rules, the project team prepare an Architecture Compliance Statement, indicating how the project complies with the specified architecture.
- This is passed to the architecture unit by change-management as the 'call' for response.
- The architecture team review the compliance-statement.
- The 'response' is either a straightforward approval, or critique and recommendations documented in a Architecture Position Statement, signalling the need for discussion and negotiation for a more architecturally-compliant solution.
- In some cases, where no architecture-compliant solution would be viable, a dispensation will be granted, documented

in an Architecture Dispensation Statement, and recorded in the dispensations-register.

- The final responsibility for the resultant go/no-go decision rests with change-management.

An apparent complication is that since we're in the process of *implementing* the first cut of the architecture, it might seem there'd be no architecture to comply with. But that's not actually the case here: we *already* have an overarching high-level architecture in the form of the agreed Business Systems and Information Systems and, higher still, the enterprise vision, values and principles: so at the very minimum we should be able to assess compliance against all of those.

The other complication is *time*: each project takes time to deliver, and during that time the architecture itself may perhaps have moved on. It's essential to keep active projects aware of any architecture-changes – something we look at in more detail in the next Phase, but which we also need especially to put into practice here.

Document the results in accordance with the applicable change-governance rules, and sign-off the architecture approval part of the gateway-review, to allow the project to move to the next stage of implementation.

Phase H: conduct 'lessons-learned' from rationalisation

Once the change-programme and its projects are complete, the architecture unit can no longer influence that aspect of the usage of architecture. But there are two tasks still to do within the architecture-cycle: identify and verify the benefits gained, and review any changes and other lessons-learned, to drive the architecture onward. The responsibility here reverts to the architecture-unit: this is primarily under architecture-governance, not change-governance, though the latter should certainly be involved.

More TOGAF: the ADM specification does describe some of the activities that need to happen here, but as usual with far too much of an IT-centric slant, and also with the assumption that there's only ever one architecture-cycle happening at once – and a very large, long cycle at that. Which isn't what happens in real-world architecture...

Practical issues such as staffing-constraints suggest that at this stage you'll probably still be doing smaller single architecture-cycles – the rationalisations for each Business System and its Information System, probably one at a time, in priority sequence – but it's best to plan for the simultaneous-cycle case right from the start, because it'll start to happen as soon as you've done even a small number of cycles. When you do this, Phase H changes from being a distinct phase in each cycle, to something more like a regular review-meeting in which benefits-realisation and lessons-learned apply to whatever work has been completed in the intervening period. It's just a governance and process issue, though: the activities and scope should remain exactly the same, whichever way you do it.

Benefits-realisation and lessons-learned

Assessments of benefits-realisation and lessons-learned follow the same general pattern, typified by those four questions of the US Army's 'After Action Review':

- What was supposed to happen?
- What actually happened?
- What was the source of the difference?
- What can we learn from this, to do differently next time?

For benefits-realisation, reframe these questions as:

- What business-value was this architecture-cycle expected to deliver?
- What was the actual value delivered? - in what terms, and according to what value-metrics?
- In what ways do these differ? What expected benefits were *not* achieved, and with what difference? What unexpected benefits *were* achieved, and with what difference? In what ways did the *form* of delivered benefit differ from that expected? In what ways - if any - did the expectations change after the initial assessment of intended benefits in Phase A? In which Phases did these expectations change?
- In what ways should these differences change how benefits-expectations are defined, monitored and measured? In what ways does this change the effective meaning of 'business value'? In what ways should processes and practice change in order to enhance the probability of achieving or exceeding the required business-benefits from future architecture-cycles?

Document the results of the benefits-realisation assessment, and publish as appropriate.

The phrase 'publish or perish' has an all too literal meaning here: architecture often seems abstract, so you *need* people to know what you've achieved, in concrete business terms. Don't skip this step!

For the architecture itself, frame the lessons-learned questions as follows:

- What was the intended architectural outcome of the cycle, as defined in Phase A?

- What actual architectural outcomes have been achieved, up to this point in the cycle? What risks, issues and dispensations have been resolved? What new risks, opportunities and issues have been identified, and new dispensations allowed?
- What were the sources of any differences between intended and actual outcomes?
- From these differences, and from the list of any outstanding risks, opportunities, issues and dispensations, what new architecture work is implied? Overall, in what ways should processes and practice change, to enhance the probability of achieving the intended outcomes of future architecture-cycles?

> The TOGAF specification for this Phase also includes a review of technology-changes, business-changes and so on in the wider context, in terms of their impact on the enterprise architecture. That review-work does indeed need to be done, and preferably on a regular basis, but it probably fits better as a distinct architecture-cycle in its own right, rather than as part of the Phase H lessons-learned process here.

Document each prospective item of future architecture work as a formal Request for Architecture Work, for review by the architecture sponsor and architecture lead, and any other stakeholders as appropriate.

Document in the respective registers any risks, opportunities or issues identified during this assessment, and assign appropriate follow-on actions. Every allowed dispensation is also in itself an architectural risk, and should be noted accordingly, with assigned review-dates and the like.

> *Important*: To ensure proper governance, the architecture cycle must *not* be signed off as complete until any required actions arising from the risks, opportunities and issues registers have been defined, assigned and approved.

Once all of the above is finalised, get the architecture-cycle signed off as complete, in accordance with the architecture-governance procedures.

Then turn to the next item in the architecture priority-list, and define its scope and stakeholders and so on in a new Phase A, to start the architecture cycle over again.

Guiding the process of change

The ***purpose*** of this section is to work alongside programme- and portfolio-management to bring change-projects into line with the new architecture.

> To do this, you'll need some kind of architecture already in place. For most people it'll probably start to make sense only when the rationalisations for one or more Business Systems are already complete, but it *is* possible to do useful alignment just with the minimal architecture implied by the enterprise values and principles, and the Business Systems and Information Systems overview-models. Do what you can to get started, anyway, and certainly the sooner the better in terms of demonstrating architecture's real business value.

On the ***people*** side, we at last move into real *practical* architecture, with the requisite skillsets to match. Once again it'll probably start with an IT emphasis, but do be ready to push outward beyond those bounds wherever appropriate and practicable.

> One of the more annoying realities of early-maturity architecture is that almost all of the work will be IT-oriented – not because the need for cross-mode integration between IT-based, manual and machine-based processes doesn't exist, but more because most people won't even understand what that integration *is*, let alone how to do it. IT-folk in particular are often *very* uncomfortable about looking anywhere outside of their own domain: hence the absurd IT-centrism in TOGAF, FEAF and so many of the other 'enterprise'-architecture frameworks.
>
> But whether we like it or not, this inherent myopia *is* a fundamental fact of 'the trade': if we try to fight against it, or force our way past it – the classic mistake of 'playing architecture police' – all we'll do is make things worse. People will 'get it' – architecturally speaking – only when they're ready to 'get it', when they see that it's to *their* advantage to 'get it': our job here is to provide conditions in which they *can* 'get it', and help them see the wider view wherever we can.

Strong links with the Programme Management Office or its equivalent will be crucial to the take-up of architecture. Not only will you need them to involve you in their reviews at each project 'gateway', but you'll also need their active cooperation to catch the attention of project teams at the earliest possible moment - preferably before the final requirements phase, and certainly before any ideas about 'solutions' have become too fixed.

One essential difference between this and the previous section is that the architecture unit has only the one role, as architecture advisor - not as 'client' for the respective project. So the stakeholder relationships here are radically different from those of before: the architecture unit will have important responsibilities, yet often - especially in early-maturity architecture - quite limited authority. Good negotiating skills and limitless reserves of quiet patience will be essential attributes here!

For *planning,* much of the work will driven by the call-and-response of the Architecture Compliance Statement and Position Statement, but it's likely that there will also be extensive need for 'what-if' models to show architecture implications and design options in different development scenarios.

> A good architecture-toolset will really start to show its worth here: it's certainly possible to do all the models in standard office drawing-software such as PowerPoint or Visio, of course, but by the time you've drawn the nineteenth minor variation of version twenty-six of some system overview, the phrase "there *must* be a better way to do this" will be beginning to make itself felt!
>
> Be warned that not all the toolsets have good version-management,: but it's something you'll really need at this point – so make sure you check for it when evaluating toolsets for your needs.

The *practice* revolves around engagement and providing architectural advice, mainly in the architecture support-activities in the project-management equivalents of Phases E to G in the standard architecture cycle. The required actions are summarised below under the respective activities-headings.

For *performance,* the key business outcome is improved overall effectiveness from alignment to the new architecture, consolidating and extending the gains from the rationalisations to date. The main architecture artefacts will be diagrams and models to assist in project planning and system-design, and governance documents such as the Architecture Compliance Statement, Position Statement and Dispensation Statement.

Assist in defining requirements for change (Phases A-D)

Working with the Programme Management Office, identify all upcoming projects which touch the scope currently covered by the architecture. Set out to build personal connections with the key players and stakeholders in each project, to find out their probable architecture needs and possible architecture impact. Use the Function Model and the derived Business System and Information System models to identify other project developments in the same space, pointing to potential for architecture clashes or for cross-project synergies.

> This 'early-warning' process may seem tedious, especially in early-maturity architecture, but the effort in building personal connections with developers and project-teams does deliver huge payoffs in the longer term, particularly in terms of trust.

> Sometimes it can also deliver huge dividends in the short-term, too. In one client, we were able to catch what would have been a truly horrible clash between systems, just before the key project committed themselves to a multi-million-dollar contract; in another, we were able to show how the combined business-value of half a dozen major projects could be almost doubled by a few minor adjustments to the scope and interfaces of a small 'glue'-project that few people before had believed had any merit at all. If you want to prove the real worth of enterprise architecture, all you need do is keep your eyes open – and keep talking, keep listening, keep building that engagement with others.

For the scoping phase of projects (as for Phase A), for example:

- Use the framework layers (see p.14) to help identify responsibilities and timescales
- Use the framework columns (see p.15) to help distinguish between process, function, capability, service, events and the like
- Use the framework segments (see p.15) to help clarify asset- and location-types and the types of capabilities, functions and decisions needed to work with each
- Use the respective framework cells to help identify stakeholders and owners for each item and item-type in scope

In the 'as-is' and 'to-be' assessment phases for projects (equivalent of Phases B and C):

- Use the architecture repository to identify relevant items in scope for the current and preferred-future time-horizons, and create architecture context-models as appropriate
- Use the requirements, risks and opportunities, issues and dispensations registers to identify any architectural concerns which may be in scope
- Use the Glossary and Thesaurus to guide item-naming and identify any potential naming-conflicts

> The ArchiMate® modelling language may prove particularly useful here. Developed in the Netherlands, it's the enterprise IT-architect's equivalent of the software-architect's UML Unified Modelling Language, and is important not only because it has *some* grasp of a world beyond IT, but perhaps more because it emphasises the links between the layers as much as the entities within the layers themselves.
>
> Most model-types describe interactions only within a single framework layer – such as BPMN Business Process Modelling Notation – or perhaps aim to model the transactions between two layers within a single framework column – as in logical-to-physical data-transforms. By

contrast, ArchiMate manages to cover almost all of the framework, from row-2 Business to row-5 Deploy, and some or most aspects of every column. It does have some significant limitations – in its current form, for example, it has only limited reference to the people-aspects of architecture, and almost no reference to machine-processes outside of IT – but these *are* acknowledged, and *are* being addressed.

ArchiMate is now supported by an increasing number of architecture toolsets, and has recently been adopted by the Open Group for promotion as a formal architecture standard; more information at www.archimate.org and www.opengroup.org/archimate . Recommended.

In the gap-analysis phase for projects (equivalent of Phase D):

- Use the gap-analysis process (as described in the previous section - see p.78) to summarise known architectural gaps within the project scope
- Use the requirements, issues, risks and opportunities registers to reiterate any architectural concerns which may be in scope
- Use the dispensation registers to identify any dispensations in scope which could potentially be resolved by the project
- Create links as appropriate between the architecture-requirements register and the project's own requirements-register, and likewise for risks, opportunities and issues

Remember that the architecture unit has only an advisory role in this context, not a design or compliance role.

Assist in solution-architecture (Phase E)

This is essentially the same as in the transition from requirements to solution-architecture in the Business System rationalisation (see p.80), but in an advisory role only.

There will probably be even more of an emphasis here on dispensations: seeking ways to resolve old ones, and preventing the proliferation of new ones.

The latter – preventing proliferation of private point-solutions – is likely to be a constant source of struggles in the IT context! On one side, IT-folks do seem to like to play with the 'new toys' of technology wherever possible, and may well bend the requirements to fit the latest technology fad – the classic 'cart before the horse'. To be fair, though, the sheer complexity of IT, and the rather large gap between what's required and what IT-vendors can actually deliver, means that the ideal world defined by the Business Systems is often unachievable in practice. Hence the need for dispensations: solutions that go against the architecture, but still have to be allowed to go ahead anyway.

> The point here is not that a dispensation is 'wrong' as such, but that it represents an architecture risk. Every time we allow a dispensation, we're increasing organisational risk; every time we resolve a dispensation, we're reducing that risk. So it's not about architectural 'purity', it's about management of organisational risk. If you frame it that way round, you'll probably find that even the most IT-obsessed of folk will become more willing to cooperate here.

Assist in detailed project-design (Phase F)

Much the same applies when acting as architectural advisor in the project detailed-design phase: use the same questions as in the respective part of the Business System rationalisation (see p.81).

As maturity develops, involvement of the architecture unit should become routine, as an explicit part of the project- or programme-management cycle. Until then, use whatever contacts are available to connect with ongoing projects - and, more important, to gain their trust for the longer term.

Review and advise in project implementation (Phase G)

These activities would be under standard change-programme governance, via the call-and-response at each project-governance gateway (see p.82).

> Unlike the Business System rationalisation, this is not your project going through implementation here: so this will only work if you've already created the formal links into the programme-governance processes. To do that, you'll need sufficient authority behind you – which at this scope will usually mean someone at CxO level. Which is why you really do need someone at that level as your sponsor, right from the very beginning. In governance, that authority *matters*.

This aspect of architecture demands a delicate balance between determination and diplomacy: we need projects to comply with the architecture, but we also need project-teams to feel that they *own* the results, that compliance is something they've *chosen*, rather than forced upon them by a meddling 'architecture police'. Technical skills and knowledge also matter here, to provide suggestions about design and synergy that would be genuinely useful for projects - and those ideas *must* be meaningful if the architecture team is to build the long-term credibility it needs.

Review 'lessons-learned' from project (Phase H)

Once implementation is complete, work with the project-team and, probably, the quality unit of the change-governance body, to identify business-benefits gained and lessons-learned, both for the broader business context, and specifically for further development of the architecture. For the latter, ensure that this review includes the architecture concerns addressed at the end of each Business System rationalisation (see p.84).

> Again, this is not your project, so you'll need cooperation from the project-team in order to identify business-value and lessons-learned for the architecture. Which again brings us back to the importance of those relationship-building and negotiation skills – because they'll be essential if we're to be able to win others' active cooperation in this.

On completion, document and publish the results as before, noting any potential Requests for Architecture Work; and refer back to the change-management body for pointers to any other projects which might be able to use architectural assistance.

Resources

- 🕮 Adapting TOGAF for whole-of-enterprise scope: see Tom Graves, *Bridging the Silos: enterprise architecture for IT-architects* (Tetradian, 2008)
- 🕸 TOGAF (The Open Group Architecture Framework): see www.opengroup.org/architecture/togaf9-doc/arch/
- 🕮 Business 'operating model' and enterprise IT-architecture: see Jeanne W. Ross, Peter Weill and David C. Robertson, *Enterprise Architecture as strategy: creating a foundation for business execution* (Harvard Business School Press, 2006)
- 🕮 Enterprise-architecture as a service-oriented architecture: see Tom Graves, *The Service Oriented Enterprise: enterprise architecture and viable services* (Tetradian, 2009)
- 🕸 ArchiMate architecture modelling language: see www.archimate.org and www.opengroup.org/archimate

STEP 3: STRATEGY AND STUFF

At the start of this step we have a fully-structured architecture in live use - or at least a well-defined part of that architecture, as a bounded set of Business Systems - and some solid experience in guiding projects to align with that architecture. In short, we have repeatable processes, for repeatable business outcomes. We now need to extend this with defined mechanisms to cope with *change*: at this stage as response to variance in strategy, law and the like, though later also able to react to real-time events as well.

Purpose and strategy: The focus here is on '***top-down***' themes such as compliance management and impact of strategic change.

> This is the kind of work where TOGAF should come into its prime, on the second and subsequent ADM cycles. Which it sort-of does, as long as we assume an entirely IT-centric world...
>
> To make sense of what we *ought* to be able to do with TOGAF, first strip out all of its inappropriate IT-centrism; then its assumption that we can't do anything until we've analysed everything in Zachman's 'excruciating detail'; and also its assumption that every architecture assessment must lead to a major portfolio of projects. You'll then end up with something that *can* tackle top-down issues in any business context – which is what we have here.
>
> Just note that whilst this is where TOGAF stops, we don't. This is still only Step Three out of five or more: there's a lot of valuable work to do here, but even when we've done it, we can still develop our architecture – and its business value – much further than this.

People and governance: During this stage the architecture team may well need to grow rapidly in size and range of skillsets, to cover the broader scope and depth and sheer *scale* of the work. (At a later point the team will start to shrink again, as specialist teams are split off or attached to specific long-term projects: that process may start to happen in the later parts of this stage, though it gains pace more in the next.) At the start, the dominant skillsets will be in different aspects of IT - technology, applications, data, security, security, networks and so on - but by the end will need to include legal, compliance, quality-assurance and a myriad of other skills related to the specific business domain.

The general approach to governance will remain the same as in the previous step, but there will need to be changes as time goes on, to establish architecture as an explicit bridge between strategy and change-management. Architecture typically starts out as a pilot-project in one specific area of the business such as some aspect of IT: during this step its reach will need to extend outward both *vertically* - upward to strategy, downward to detailed operations - and *horizontally* - across silos and business domains - and its governance will likely need amendment to reflect each change in scope and authority.

> One of the defining characteristics of maturity for the end of this step is that, like any other form of enterprise-wide quality-management, architecture has explicit global reach and global authority throughout the organisation. Within its own specific terms of reference, of course: no matter how much we might wish otherwise, architecture does not rule the business world! But that breadth *is* the scope that's needed: and hence the need for matching forms of governance, too.

The other key governance theme here is that since we'll be dealing with change, for strategy and the like, we will also need to define governance for managing the *process* of changes to the architecture itself.

Planning and frameworks: The Business System rationalisations should have resulted in a standardised set of architecture models that describe required structures right the way across the IT scope at least. In this step we'll expand the 'bindedness' of those structures across an increasing breadth and depth of the enterprise scope, working towards a full set of reference-models for the over-all architecture.

> Wherever practicable, these reference-models should draw on existing standards, for specific domains – such as TOGAF's Integrated Information Infrastructure Reference Model and Technical Reference Model, for the IT domain – and for your industry or business – such as the eTOM model for telecoms, or FEAF's Performance Reference Model for US federal agencies. In each case, though, you'll need to adapt those reference-models for your own specific context: aligning to a standard is useful, because it gives you a means to compare and communicate with others, but there will always be some aspects that will be unique to your enterprise alone.

Practice and methods: For consistency, use the standard Agile-style architecture development cycle (see p.20) throughout all sections of the work.

> The detailed methods will vary with each type of work and context, of course. The TOGAF specification provides a good overview of the methods you'll need for each type of conventional IT-architecture – the classic set of IT-infrastructure architecture, applications-architecture, data architecture and IT-related aspects of business-

architecture, plus a few hints at security and service-architecture – and as long as you strip out the IT-centrism, it provides a fair indication of what general types of activities would be needed outside of the IT domain.

Perhaps more important than any overt activity, though, is a specific mindset: a way of enquiring, exploring, engaging, taking ideas apart and recombining them in unexpected ways, an ability to hold the big-picture in mind whilst diving down into the depths. That's the *real* method of architecture: the rest is just detail, really. Important detail, non-trivial detail, but just detail nonetheless.

Performance, end-products and metrics: There's no set timescale for any of the work in this step: by now - or certainly during this step - the architecture should be fully established as an ongoing strategic capability for the business, with the sections listed here just typical examples of the tasks that would be undertaken. The one point to reiterate here is that *every item of architecture work starts with an explicit business purpose, for explicit business value* - and defining business-value would include defining any required timetables and milestones and deliverables and so on.

As in the previous step, typical artefacts would include:

- architecture-models, of a much broader range of model-types, and across a broader scope
- TOGAF-style 'roadmaps' or 'blueprints'
- requirements, risk-assessments, reports, and other architecture-engagement artefacts

But again, the most important outcomes will be invisible, if on the surface at least: the dialogue, the engagement of others in the pervasive *idea* of architecture as a practice within the entire enterprise - which in itself is a key driver to pull the architecture maturity onward.

Expand outward from IT

The ***purpose*** of this section is to identify dependencies across the whole enterprise - rather than solely or primarily across IT - so as to be able to track potential impacts of strategic and other change.

On the ***people*** side, most of this will be business-analysis again, but now will need to be able go much deeper into the operations-layer if needed. And for much of this work you will *definitely* need that high-level authority and support, because by the time it's complete you will have had to bridge across every single silo-boundary in the enterprise.

For ***planning***, the start-point will be the Business Systems and Information Systems models again, usually moving back upward to the Function Model, and outward again from there.

> If you haven't already extended the detailed Business Systems models to include the flows of physical 'things' and other non-information assets, you should probably do so anyway as part of this work. For each asset-type, aim also to build an equivalent of the Information System model (see p. 71): it's unlikely that there would be an exact analogue of the information-management 'single source of truth', but otherwise the principles – and the questions that need to be asked – are much the same.

By this stage you *must* also have a proper architecture-toolset in place and in use. The sheer complexity of all the interconnections between entities, requirements, risks and so on, is far beyond the capability of standard office software: don't even *think* of trying to limp along here with a couple of spreadsheets and a home-made database, because it'll drive you mad in days.

The ***practice*** would again use the standard architecture cycle..

> In principle, anyway: the catch is that much of this work actually has to happen *inside* other architecture-support projects, because in itself it often doesn't have direct *visible* business value. The value is real, but at this stage most people outside of architecture won't see the point until the information is already in place and in use. More on this below.

Breaking away from 'architecture as project', ***performance*** here would begin to be measured more in terms of its service-delivery: speed of response, appropriateness of response, value added as a result of the response, and so on. The challenge here is that of *relevance*: all those architectural artefacts we'll produce here are interesting, no doubt, but it's up to us to make them relevant in real everyday business practice.

The enterprise as whole

In most cases, enterprise architecture starts out in IT. But although most descriptions still assume it's solely about IT, in reality it just doesn't work that way: everything connects with everything else. We can see this clearly in the history of enterprise architecture:

- to make the technology effective, we need to understand the applications that run on it
- to make the applications effective, we need to understand the data managed by them

- to make the data useful as business information, we need to understand the business drivers and strategies
- to make sense of the business drivers and strategies, we need to understand the *enterprise* – the organisation's role, market and compliance context

That sequence brings us to the scope of the current versions of TOGAF and FEAF, for example. But that sequence still has its roots in IT: and at the operational level, it doesn't really tell us much about anything *other* than IT. So we also need to work our way back *down* the same sequence, to make sense of the enterprise as a whole:

- the market context defines the reasons for the business drivers and strategies
- the drivers and strategies imply capabilities and services
- the capabilities and services imply processes and functions
- the processes and functions imply concrete implementations in the real world

Which brings us back to physical IT again: servers and networks and routers and laptops and mobiles and disks and all the other IT paraphernalia. But it *also* brings us down to manual processes, and skills of individual people, and photocopiers and fork-lift trucks – which, from an architectural perspective, also need to be managed and monitored and modelled in an exactly consistent way.

Which brings us back to the rows and columns and segments of the framework (see p.13), and the reason why the architecture development method (see p.20) *doesn't* assume TOGAF's fixed IT-centric scope, but instead allows any scope to be specified at the start of the architecture cycle, drawn from the architecture framework. The architecture of the enterprise is a holograph:

Everything in the enterprise depends on everything else.

Which means that we need to embed that awareness within the architecture process. So although most the work at this stage will probably still be IT-oriented, the way to embed that wider awareness is to note every point where IT touches a non-IT space. Then, instead of ignoring that connection – which is what happens far too often at present in most IT-architecture – make it explicit in the architecture-repository, and follow the trails of connections for at least one or two steps beyond the initial contact-point. If we do that, we'll then have the 'hooks' in place to explore further –

which we'll need to be able to do in the next section, when we start to look at the impacts of strategy.

Extending the scope-awareness

The IT domain is typically bounded by applications (composites of virtual *capability* and virtual *function*), data (virtual *assets*) and IT infrastructure (physical *assets* assigned to composites of physical and virtual *locations*), with processes typically triggered by signals or messages (composites of virtual *events* and virtual *assets*). The primitives and composites of the enterprise space outside of that domain – the 'non-IT space' – may incorporate any of those framework 'cells', and will certainly include all of the other 'cells'. So at each contact-point with a non-IT space during conventional IT-oriented architecture assessments, further questions could include:

- At what framework *layer* does this touch-point occur? What are the implied responsibilities and time-perspectives here?
- What are the transactions at this touch-point? What types of *functions*, *assets* and *locations* are involved – *physical*, *virtual*, *relational*, or whatever? If as patterns or composites, what are their underlying primitives?
- What types of *events* – as *physical*, *virtual*, *relational* or whatever – trigger each transaction? If as patterns of composites – perhaps with specific types of assets – what are their underlying primitives?
- For each transaction, what *capabilities* are required – *physical*, *virtual*, *relational* or whatever? What competencies and skill-levels are required for these capabilities – *rule-based*, *analytic*, *heuristic*, *principle-based*? In what ways are these capabilities and skill-levels clustered into roles? In what ways do these roles intersect with the functions, assets, locations and events of the transaction?
- What *decisions* or *reasons* guide the interactions and transactions at this touch-point? How would you categorise the form of each decision – as *rules*, as outcomes of *analysis*, as guidelines or *heuristics*, or as *principles*?
- What business-principles and other principles apply in the context of this touch-point and its transactions? How does the touch-point ensure compliance with those principles? How and in what ways do these anchor back to the core principles, values and vision of the enterprise, and by what means could this compliance be verified?

Document the results in the architecture-repository - and models, if appropriate - and include any namings, risks, opportunities, issues or requirements in the respective registers.

> Be careful to keep this within realistic bounds: don't let yourself be accused of arbitrary 'scope creep', because that would really start to hurt in terms of architecture's credibility and perceived value. Focus on establishing 'hooks' for future explorations, but don't go further than that until is someone is willing to pay for it!

This goes with that

The ***purpose*** of this section is to use the architecture to identify the impacts and opportunities arising from changes in strategy, and - by running the same process in reverse - explore the strategic potential of ideas and innovations arising either within the enterprise or in the broader 'domains of interest' for the enterprise.

> The relentless creative ferment of the IT industry is one obvious 'domain of interest' for IT-architects, of course, but there will be many others for every enterprise, and each enterprise will have its own unique priorities and focus. Important innovation may come from *anywhere*, and we need to be able to notice it and respond to it when it does appear – that's really the whole point here.

On the ***people*** side, you'll need access to a much broader range of skillsets and experience for this section. These will again include the IT domain-architects, as before, but would now encompass strategists, business intelligence, market analysts and the like at the business level, process architects and any number of domain specialists at the integration and detail-levels, and the 'evangelists' who deal with the pervasive themes such as security, quality, governance, efficiency and ethics.

> As the architect, it's your task to coordinate and communicate between all of these different areas of expertise. The phrase "herding cats" may come to mind at this point... – but this is one of the most engaging and exciting areas of all of the architecture, so it's well worth the effort.

The process can go both ways, top-down or bottom-up, so for ***planning*** you'll need a toolset that can follow the trails of relationships and dependencies in either direction - or any direction, really. The toolset will also need good support for 'what-if' scenarios, and also good version-management to keep track of all those different scenarios and options.

The content for the planning that underpins the scenarios would come from the domain-specialists: your task is more to provide a means to manage the complexity of options and interrelations – the "body of knowledge about enterprise structure and purpose".

The *practice* should follow the standard architecture-development cycle. The strategy, innovation or whatever would be specified as the 'business question' in an initial Request for Architecture Work; the assessment section (Phases A to D) will often be recursive, looping back on itself as new information emerges; whilst the implementation section would consist primarily of impact reviews by subject-matter experts in other domains, from solution architects (in Phase E) to designers (in Phase F) and detail-level practitioners (in Phase G). The overall process will often be iterative, with outcomes of the Phase H review triggering new questions for new architecture-cycles.

The *performance* would be hard to measure in direct terms, because the real business-value would arrive via indirect themes such as reduced risk or reduced time-to-market. For architecture itself, though, performance should again be measured in qualitative terms such as responsiveness in service-delivery.

Strategy drives change

Here we start to make use of all those cross-dependencies and connections mapped out in the background of the work in the previous section. We start from a single high-level theme, such as a potential strategy or a potential change in law or regulation, and work our way downward through the framework to assess and design for its impact anywhere and at any level in the enterprise.

> In essence this is what the standard TOGAF stack is intended to address. We pick up the high-level theme in 'Business Architecture' (original Phase B); assess its impacts on management of business information in the data-architecture and applications-architecture reviews in 'Information-Systems Architecture' (TOGAF's Phase C); and roll on down to 'Technology Architecture' (TOGAF Phase D) to assess the impact on the IT-infrastructure. We then work out what to do about it in practice, starting with ideas for solution-designs (TOGAF Phase E).
>
> So the standard TOGAF-ADM sequence does all sort-of work if your main interest is the IT-infrastructure – which is certainly the case with most uses and users of classic TOGAF. The catch is that it doesn't really describe the sheer *messiness* of this kind of assessment, where ideas and information trigger off new information, leading to new trails that have to be followed, and so on.

A better way to understand it is that TOGAF's 'Business Architecture' is a complete architecture-iteration – or set of iterations – *in its own right*: it often goes right the way through the design-and-implementation phases, and may even end up in a place that has no IT at all. The same applies to 'Information-Systems Architecture', and 'Technology Infrastructure Architecture': each of those is drawn from a set of one of more architecture-cycles, each with their own initial business-question and business-value to start off the cycle in the respective Phase A. And again, they too may end up somewhere with no IT at all: the information-system might be a social network, and the respective technology a pin-board for shared messages. It all depends on the context.

Everything connects with everything else, 'this goes with that' – trace the trails of implied connections to identify the theme's impact on the whole.

Following the impact-trails

In a full architecture-cycle, all of this analysis - and yes, there's a lot of it - would take place in Phase B and/or Phase C, with a gap-analysis in Phase D leading to potential solution-design in Phase E, and so on. In some other cases - such as when working with a strategy-team rather than a business-transformation unit - you may need only to do the assessment itself: but do follow the usual governance rules whichever way you do it.

Start the assessment at the top-most layer of the framework (see p.14). Compare the theme against the defining ***Universals*** (row-0) for the enterprise - its vision, values and principles:

- In what ways does the theme align, or not align, with the enterprise vision, values and principles?
- If the theme represents an internal choice - such as a proposed change in strategy - what do the vision, values and principles indicate or imply about the theme? Since these, in principle, would have higher priority than a strategy, in what ways might they imply changes in the strategy?
- If the theme is imposed from the wider environment - such as a potential change in law or regulation - what do the vision, values and principles indicate or imply about organisational response to the theme? Since the vision, values and principles represent the organisation's core choices in relation to the wider environment, does the theme imply a requirement to review any of those core choices? And since these choices are fundamental to the organisation's self-definition in relation to the wider enterprise, what impact would any such changes

have on the overall structure, focus and direction of the enterprise?

Document the results of this assessment in the architecture repository in terms of impact and 'bindedness' of relationships between vision, values, principles and the respective aspects of the theme, and of any required changes to the theme itself, and also any implied risks, opportunities or issues in the respective registers.

> In each subsequent level you should again recheck each impact and implication for alignment against the vision, values and principles. In general, you would do this by comparing against the pervasive-themes – quality, security, privacy, safety and so on – which devolve from that topmost layer. If that comparison highlights a significant issue or misalignment, you may need to go back up a layer or two – perhaps even to the topmost layer – and restart the assessment with all the amendments identified to date. You never actually lose anything by going back up again, but it can be invaluable in helping you avoid intractable 'wicked problems' further down the track.

Move down the layers to follow the trails of potential impact.

At the ***Scope*** layer (row-1), identifying the key 'items of interest' for the enterprise:

- What impact would the (amended) theme have on the core assets, functions, locations, capabilities, events and decisions of the organisation?
- What impact would it have on the organisation's roles, missions and overall services and service-relationships within the enterprise?
- What impacts would it have in relation to the organisation's 'pervasives'?
- In what ways might any of these change the theme itself?

At the ***Business*** layer (row-2), where we assess the relationships between those key items:

- What impact would the (amended) theme have on the *relationships* between the core assets, functions, locations, capabilities, events and decisions of the organisation?
- What impacts would it have on relationships and transactions with other entities - other players - within the enterprise?
- What impacts would it have in relation to the organisation's 'pervasives'?
- In what ways might any of these change the theme itself?

At the ***System*** layer (row-3), where we expand those entities and their relationships out to abstract or 'logical' design-patterns that are independent of any specific implementation:

- What impacts would the (amended) theme have on the *types* - physical, virtual, relational, aspirational, abstract, composite - of assets, functions, locations, capabilities and events that would apply within the organisation's services?
- What impacts would the theme have on the *skill-levels* - rule-based, analytic, heuristic, principle-based - required for the capabilities needed within the organisation's services?
- What impacts would the theme have on the *form* and *bindedness* - rules, analyses, emergence, context-unique - required for reasons and decision-making within the organisation's services?
- What impacts would these have on *structures* of composites and design-patterns for implementations?
- What impacts would these have on *trade-offs* between implementation choices?
- What impacts would these have on *reporting-metrics* that should be consistent for all implementations of a given design-pattern?
- What impacts would these have in relation to the organisation's 'pervasives'?
- In what ways might any of these change the theme itself?

At the ***Develop*** layer (row-4), extending the abstract designs more toward the real world, with implementation-specific patterns:

- What impacts would the (amended) theme have on the *types* of assets, functions, locations, capabilities and events that would apply within an implementation?
- What impacts would the theme have on the *skill-levels* needed within an implementation?
- What impacts would the theme have on the *form* and *bindedness* for reasons and decision-making within an implementation?
- What impacts would these have on *structures* of composites for implementation-patterns?
- What impacts would these have on *trade-offs* between and within implementations?
- What impacts would these have on *reporting-metrics* and other controls within implementations?

- What impacts would these have on *transactions* and other applicable factors and concerns within implementations?
- What impacts would these have on the structures and handovers in *end-to-end processes* that use specific implementations – especially where implementations transition between human-based, machine-based and IT-based segments of end-to-end processes?
- What impacts would these have in relation to the organisation's 'pervasives'?
- In what ways might any of these change the theme itself?

At the ***Deploy*** layer (row-5), we need composites that 'complete' across all of the framework columns: "with <*asset*> do <*function*> at <*location*> using <*capability*> on <*event*> because <*reason*>". The decisions about types – physical, virtual, relational and so on – for assets and the like should all have been resolved in the previous layer; here the questions focus more on operational issues such as configuration, shift-rosters, logistics and backup-plans:

- What impacts would the (amended) theme have on planning for routine real-time *redundancy* and *variance* – overflow, underflow, task-balancing, task-mix and the like?
- What impacts would the theme have on run-time *configuration*-issues such as development versus test versus production versus fallback?
- What impacts would the theme have on planning for *maintenance* and other scheduled downtime?
- What impacts would the theme have on planning for *business-continuity*, repair, disaster-recovery and other unscheduled incidents?
- What impacts would the theme have on planning for *substitution*, rostering and other scheduled and unscheduled transfers of operational and personal responsibility?
- What impacts would the theme have on run-time *resource-management* and *reporting*?
- What impacts would the theme have on run-time *transactions* and other interactions? For what reasons, and in what ways?
- What impacts would these have in relation to the organisation's 'pervasives' – particularly run-time quality-management, security-management and legal-compliance issues?
- In what ways might any of these change the theme itself?

At the *Operations* layer (row-6), the 'complete' composites shift to the present or past-tense. Questions here need to address not only what is being done and has been done, but also in what ways these differ from the scheduled plan:

- What impacts would the (amended) theme have on *performance-reporting* and performance-metrics?
- What impacts would the theme have on *audit* and *verification* of run-time activity?
- What impacts would these have in relation to the organisation's 'pervasives' - particularly post-run-time quality-management clean-up such as correction, corrective-action and information for process-improvement?
- In what ways might any of these change the theme itself?

> To give an example for all of this, imagine you've been asked by Marketing to explore the implications to your US-based organisation of opening up an operation in south-east Asia. (The respective roles and responsibilities are clear here: you provide decision-support, but they make the final decisions on strategy.) Working with them, and starting from the top-most layer of the framework, these are some examples of questions that might come up in the conversation.
>
> *Business questions*: What would be the impact on the whole enterprise of opening operations in south-east Asia? What are the risks, opportunities and viability concerns? Which country – if any – would be the best choice to start?
>
> *Business value*: decision support leading to reduced risk and possible enhanced opportunities.
>
> ***Universals*** layer: In this context, what is the broader enterprise in which the organisation would fit? What would be the organisation's role within this enterprise? How well does this align with the organisation's own vision, values and principles for its enterprise? For example, transparency in decision-making is deemed a core principle for this enterprise, with strong compliance requirements for the US-based business: different countries have different cultures around bribery and covert deal-making, so this principle may help to prioritise the choice of start-location. The same applies to principles around diversity and other people-issues: some countries have strict rules or social sensitivities on gender-roles and organisational authority of 'outsiders', so this again should point out some specific priorities.
>
> ***Scope*** layer: What are the 'key items of interest' for the enterprise? How well do they align with the proposed market? What assets, functions, locations, capabilities, events, decisions would be required? Again, use these to prioritise countries, and perhaps particular regions or cities within countries.
>
> ***Business*** layer: What products and services would be offered within this market? Given the role within the Asian enterprise – as

determined in the 'Universals' layer – what missions would this imply? What infrastructures would be required to support those missions? How would the assets, functions, locations, capabilities, events and decisions interconnect in this Asian context, and in what ways would this differ from other markets? What risks and opportunities arise from those differences?

System layer: What processes would be required to deliver those products and services in the respective market and context? What implementations would be available for those processes? Which parts of which processes can be replicated from elsewhere in the organisation? What are the trade-offs between human-based, machine-based and IT-based process-segments and their handovers in this context? Are there any likely gaps or constraints on required assets, functions, locations, capabilities, events and decisions for this context, and if so, how would this affect the trade-offs between choices for implementations, or for choices for start-point in this market? In what ways would the trade-offs between buy, build and re-use change in this context? How do we ensure consistency in resource-management, reporting and compliance with that which applies elsewhere in the organisation?

Develop layer: What practical implications, risks and opportunities arise from the trade-offs identified in the 'System' layer? What capabilities and respective skill-levels would be needed in this context, to be able to develop and set up the required missions identified in the 'Business' layer? What gaps exist, and what do these gaps imply in terms of impact on schedules for time-to-market? What impact would context-specific concerns such as language and local legislation have on developments for this market?

Deploy layer: What workflow and market variances have to be allowed for in this context? What impacts will these have on run-time business processes? What rollback and business-continuity plans would be needed? Are the skillsets needed to operate those backup plans available in this context? What local laws and ordinances need to be addressed for operations-planning?

Operations layer: How will performance-reporting be recorded and managed? How will this reporting be aligned with standards in use elsewhere in the organisation, so as to be able to compare like-with-like? What after-the-fact follow-up will be required to resolve staffing and other operational issues, and to support quality-management and process-improvement?

A minor warning: by definition the trails go to infinity, so be realistic about how far you follow them! No matter how fascinating all those side-trails may be, don't allow yourself to get stuck in 'analysis paralysis'. The whole point of a holographic approach is that you don't have to do it all at once, and you don't *need* to try to do it all at once: if 'this goes with that', then that goes with this – you'll find yourself coming back to the same place from another direction some other time anyway. So just do what you need, when you need it, and allow the full picture to emerge as it will.

As before, document the results in the architecture repository in terms of impact and 'bindedness' of relationships between the entities at this level and the respective aspects of the theme, and of any required changes to the theme itself, and also any implied risks, opportunities or issues in the respective registers..

Innovation invokes strategy

All of the above assumes that the theme to be considered in this kind of analysis is already known. But we also need to keep an eye open at all times for useful ideas and suggestions that we *don't* know about beforehand. Such innovations could well come from *anywhere* - from the industry, the market, from new technology, from within the organisation itself, to name just a few of the possible sources. So we need systematic processes to find them and to assess their value and implications for the enterprise.

This is where business-intelligence – in the broader sense of term – aligns itself with enterprise architecture. Some aspects of this are actually included in standard TOGAF, as part of the original ADM's Phase H, but as usual it's only from an IT-centric perspective, and only happens at the end of what could well be a multi-year architecture-cycle. In the real world of business, we need something with a broader scope, something a bit more systematic, and quite a lot more frequent. So in practice, the better option is to run it as a regular architecture-cycle in its own right, as described here.

This kind of search might need to be done in any of a whole variety of ways - top-down, bottom-up, sideways-in and so on - but in practice we can tweak the standard architecture-cycle to give us a workable process for the purpose whichever way round we would want to do it. Strictly speaking it's always sort-of top-down, but it comes out the same in the end.

In ***Phase A*** we define the scope for the architecture-iteration. The business-question for the cycle is always the same - the search for appropriate innovation to enhance enterprise effectiveness - and likewise the business-value will be in terms of reduced risk, reduced time-to-market and suchlike. But we'll need to constrain the search to some suitable scope, in order to return usable results within a reasonable timescale and realistic budget.

We don't automatically ignore anything interesting that's outside of that preset scope – in fact one of the key aims of this exercise is to allow the unexpected to emerge. Instead, like an architecture principle, the scope provides a known, certain reference-point for the investigation: if we seem to be straying too far it, perhaps it's time to come back to that anchor and rethink where we're going. It doesn't prevent us from finding what we need, but it does protect us against getting lost in the uncertain seas of innovations and ideas.

In ***Phase B*** we explore the 'as-is' architecture in terms of the scope, allowing new ideas to emerge:

- What are others doing at present, in the same industry, the same overall enterprise, in other enterprises entirely? What could we learn from this?
- What technologies, business-processes, business-models and so on are others using at present? What could we use or adapt from this?
- What does benchmarking against competitors, partners, or other industries suggest?
- What gaps exist within the current architecture? What gaps do these suggest in terms of potential for innovation?
- What options and needs for innovation are indicated by risks, opportunities, issues and dispensations currently recorded in the respective registers?
- What risks, opportunities and issues do all of *these* imply for the architecture, and for the enterprise as a whole?

In ***Phase C*** we do the same for one or more future time-horizons. We ask the same questions as in the previous phase, but with more of a future-oriented emphasis, such as about upcoming technologies, known trends in the industry, and brainstorming for possible 'wild-cards' that could create or change a whole industry.

Although this does intersect with architecture here, this kind of future-forward assessment is almost a separate field in itself. We use a broad range of formal futures-tools in our own work, including scenarios (by which we mean proper multi-axis scenario-development – not the simplistic 'business scenarios' in the TOGAF specification, which are what anyone else would call business-analysis), causal-layered analysis, and environmental scanning; but the appropriate choice for your context would depend on your specific industry and needs. Groups such as the Association of Professional Futurists can help here, to point towards suitable tools, techniques and training – see www.profuturists.org for more details.

In ***Phase D*** we do a variant of the standard gap-analysis, in which we not only compare between the 'as-is' and the one or more 'to-be' views, but also record and assess any gaps and issues that we've found within each view. From this we derive a list of ideas or themes or questions that we could then bring to others for their opinions.

In ***Phase E*** we share and explore this list with solution-architects, process-architects and high-level designers. Although we're not doing any solution-design as such, these are the same people that we would work with in developing solution-architectures and the like, so we can re-use the same stakeholder-lists and governance-rules for this purpose. What we're looking for here are potential innovations in the solution-architecture space, as per the chosen scope but across the whole enterprise: examples would include new design-patterns, new development-processes, new technologies and so on. We're also looking for their views on risks and other issues, as seen from their own communities of practice that bridge beyond the enterprise itself. Document these - usually in the respective risks, opportunities or issues registers - and also add them to the discussion-list as appropriate.

> Note that not only are we working with specific stakeholder-groups in each phase, we're also in effect working our way down the framework layers: the stakeholders in Phase E typically work at the boundary between 'System' (row-3) and 'Develop' (row-4); those in Phase F go from there down to 'Deploy' (row-5); and those in Phase G also tackle real-world issues in 'Operations' (row-6).

In ***Phase F*** we do the same with developers, detail-level designers and project-managers - again, much the same groups of people with whom we would usually work in this phase of a normal architecture development-cycle. Here we look for innovations in planning and preparation, new combinations of ideas and options that have direct practical applications; and likewise, their views on risks, opportunities and other potential issues. Again, document these as appropriate.

In ***Phase G*** we move much closer to the real-world processes and transactions of the enterprise. Typical themes that would arise with the people who work in these contexts would include new ideas in workflow-management, quality-management, business-continuity and disaster-recovery; again, they too have their own communities of practice both within and beyond the organisation, and their hands-on experience makes them more likely than most to spot any potential for *practical* innovation.

In ***Phase H,*** working with the sponsor for the overall review, we pull together all the different strands that have come up throughout the architecture-cycle, to produce a prioritised list of strategic themes.

> Remember that a so-called 'solution' is not a strategy! A 'solution' is something that a vendor wants to sell, and is almost invariably designed to fit someone else's needs – sometimes only the vendor's needs, to be somewhat cynical about it...
>
> Remember the rigid rule here: anything that purports to be a 'solution' to something must be shelved until Phase E at the earliest in any architecture-cycle: prior to that point, we *only* assess requirements. So when we come across a purported 'solution' in this type of work, note it down, place it ready to go into the Phase E of a suitable cycle, and search for the real needs and issues *behind* that 'solution', that it would aim to address. The relevant strategic theme that we would use as the initiating 'business question' for an architecture-cycle would typically be at least two or three steps back from any would-be 'solution', and will usually be much broader in scope: it's that business-question that we're looking for here in this kind of review.

As advised by the sponsor, develop each appropriate theme as a Request for Architecture Work, to carry forward either via the strategy-assessment process as above (see p.101) or as a standard architecture cycle for a change-project (see p. 73).

Abstract-services

The ***purpose*** of this section is two-fold: to clarify the trade-offs between different implementations of what is in effect the same service; and, from the opposite direction, identify common factors between implementations, such as reporting-metrics that would simplify comparing like-with-like under different operating conditions. To do these, we first need to identify what that common implementation-independent 'abstract service' is in each case.

> If you've come to enterprise-architecture from an IT-architecture background, part of the purpose here is to help you break free from any habit of thinking about implementations only in IT-centric terms. Coming from a single domain, it's common to think that all solutions depend on that domain: hence, in turn, the tendency of IT-architects to assume that every problem has an IT-based solution, and that the IT solution is *necessarily* the best option *because* it is IT-based. Reality is that there *isn't* always an IT solution, and even where an IT solution is available, it may not be the most *effective* solution – for example, the optimal solution for a specific inter-team communication context might be a humble pin-board rather than an expensive and potentially-fragile IT-based messaging-system. Enhancing the architect's ability to understand those trade-offs and identify the most optimal solutions for a range of different contexts is one of the key aims here.

> Although this is most often a concern for former IT-architects, the same also applies to other architects too – for example, business-architects may tend to think in people-centric terms, and ignore the possibilities for IT-based decision-support. Either way, use this section to get into a habit of thinking in terms of trade-offs, rather than reflexively in terms of a single type or category of implementations.

On the ***people*** side, you'll need relations with people who develop and manage the different respective types of implementations for the service; with people who need those common performance-metrics; and probably also with the 'evangelists' and practitioners of the key 'pervasives' in scope.

The ***planning*** would draw from the Function Model (see p.49) and Business System and Information System models (see p.67), and their equivalents for other asset-types and asset-flows (see p.95).

> Ideally, you should by now have function-models down to tier-4 for the respective scope, but if not you'll be collecting the requisite information during this work anyway.

The ***practice*** should follow the usual architecture-cycle: note that it's likely that change-projects would arise from this work, so it'll include an emphasis on the implementation-oriented second half of the cycle.

Some of the ***performance*** can be measured in terms of direct cost-savings - especially where trade-offs can identify lower-cost yet still optimal service-architecture solutions. This is also important in setting the groundwork for business-continuity and disaster-recovery planning. The most visible business-benefit, though, will be from enabling and establishing like-for-like comparisons across multiple implementations - typical in load-balancing, or between different regions or countries, or again in disaster-recovery - which would make the decision-tasks of managers and executives a whole lot easier. You can affirm the business worth of enterprise architecture, beyond any future doubt, on this one point alone - so it's important to put the extra effort into this to get it right.

Technologies and trade-offs

We looked briefly at services some while ago (see p.48), and we'll come back to them again in more detail later (see p.143); for here, we'll use the same architectural principle that *everything in the enterprise is a service*. Each of the business-functions delivers a service; coordination of end-to-end processes is a service; change-management is a service; management itself is a service. *Everything* is a service.

A *service* is a composite of *function* - a point where an identified change can take place - and *capability* - a set of competencies to enact the required change. We combine function together with a different capability or technology to deliver a different service. (A 'technology' is a clustering-together of a specific set of capabilities, so the term fits well enough here.) Conversely, the same function can be implemented in many different ways and with different technologies:

A function may be implemented by any combination of machine-based, IT-based or human-based capabilities.

A direct analogue here is the old gardener's Soil Types Diagram. In principle, any type of soil can be described in terms of a combination of three different materials - clay, sand and silt. Because these are mutually exclusive - more clay in the mix means that there must be less of sand or silt - we can describe these three axes in just two dimensions with a triangular layout. So we can use the same format to describe the three implementation dimensions.

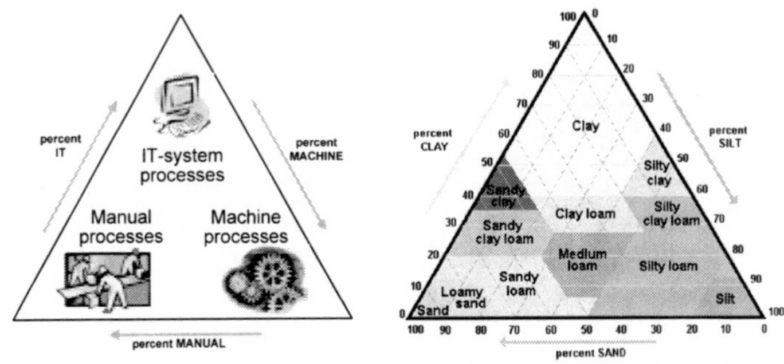

Service-types and soil-types: different mixes for different needs

But in order to assess the *trade-offs* between different implementations, and to create meaningful metrics, we also need to be able to describe the commonalities between these services. This set of commonalities - the 'outside view' of the function, the bounding triangle on that service-types diagram - is somewhat confusingly termed a 'business service', or abstract service.

There's a fairly close analogy here with the Object Management Group's 'Model Driven Architecture' (MDA), originally developed for IT-architecture but currently being enhanced and adapted to apply to the broader scope of enterprise architecture. In MDA terms, the abstract-service at a tier-4 level would be a 'Platform Independent Model' (PIM), while each implementation would be a 'Platform-Specific Model' (PSM). Going up the Function Model to tier-3 and above, we would also move up a notch in the MDA: the abstract-service there would be analogous to an MDA 'Computation-Independent Model' (CIM), whilst its expression – usually as a tier-4 abstract-service – would be the PIM.

Architecturally, then, we first need to assess the business-service in the abstract, to identify the common requirements that each implementation must be able to deliver; and then look at options and trade-offs for different implementations, to identify the best fit for each different context.

Services in abstract

Viewing the function in scope as an abstract 'business service':

- What does the service *do*? What is its purpose within the overall enterprise? What value does it deliver?
- What *assets* would be used or referenced within the abstract service? - that would be common to *every* implementation of the service? Are these assets physical, virtual, relational, abstract or other composite forms?
- In what *locations* would the abstract-service be delivered? What types of locations are involved in delivery of the service? Are these locations physical, virtual, relational, abstract or other composite forms?
- What *events* trigger or are triggered by the services? What types of events are involved in delivery of the service? Are these events physical, virtual, relational, abstract or other composite forms?
- What *decisions* and *business-rules* apply to and within the abstract-service? What types of decisions are involved? Are these decisions rule-based, analytic, emergent, principle-based or other composite forms?
- What *capabilities*, and *competencies* of those capabilities, would be required to deliver the abstract-service? In what ways do the asset-types, location-types and event-types - physical, virtual, relational, aspirational, abstract and composite - and decision-types - rule-based, analytic, emergent, principle-based - determine the capability-types and competencies that would be required in every implementation of the service?
- In *interfaces* to the abstract-service, either as 'requester' for the service, or 'provider' to the service, what would be required

that is common to every implementation of the service? What are the assets, events and information-flows that would be required in each transaction? What content would be required for a service-level agreement for each interface?

- In what business-processes is the abstract-service used? By what means is the use of the service *coordinated* or choreographed with other services to deliver the results of each business-process?
- In what way is the overall abstract-service managed? What *control-information* and *performance-metrics* would be common to every implementation of the service?
- What determines *quality* within the abstract-service? How would such quality be monitored and maintained within every implementation of the service?

The results would define requirements that should be common to *all* implementations of this abstract business-service.

> Note that the required competencies – skill-levels or equivalent – for the capabilities will be critical in determining trade-offs between implementations. In practice, machines can only be used to implement rule-based capabilities, and IT only for rule-based and analytic: in general, IT can be used for decision-*support* in emergent and principle-based contexts, but not for decision-*making* – a crucial distinction which is all too often forgotten in practice! Conversely, although people *can* do work which is solely rule-based, the presence of *some* scope for personal skill is essential to engagement, because personal effectiveness will suffer without it: wherever practicable, rule-only components of work should be implemented by machines or by IT.

Document the results as entities, attributes and links in architecture models, and as requirements, risks, opportunities and issues in the appropriate repositories, with any names and cross-references entered in the glossary and thesaurus.

Services for real

For each potential implementation of the abstract-service:

- What does the implementation *do* internally that implements the abstract-service? What additional value – if any – does it deliver?
- What additional *assets* would be used or referenced within the service-implementation? – that would be specific to *this* implementation of the service? Does the implementation itself impose constraints on the assets and asset-types that can be

used? Are these assets physical, virtual, relational, abstract or other composite forms?

- In what additional *locations* would the implementation be delivered? What additional types of locations are involved in delivery of the service? Does the implementation itself impose constraints on the locations and location-types that are involved? Are these locations physical, virtual, relational, abstract or other composite forms?
- What additional *events* trigger or are triggered by the implementation? What types of events are involved in delivery of the service? Does the implementation itself impose constraints on the events and event-types that are involved? Are these events physical, virtual, relational, abstract or other composite forms?
- What additional *decisions* and *business-rules* apply to and within the implementation? What types of decisions are involved? Does the implementation itself impose constraints on the decisions and decision-types that are involved? Are these decisions rule-based, analytic, emergent, principle-based or other composite forms?
- What additional *capabilities*, and *competencies* of those capabilities, would be required to deliver the implementation? In what ways do the asset-types, location-types and event-types - physical, virtual, relational, aspirational, abstract and composite - and decision-types - rule-based, analytic, emergent, principle-based - determine the capability-types and competencies that would be required? Does the implementation itself impose constraints on the capabilities and competencies that would be required to deliver the service?
- In *interfaces* to the abstract-service, either as 'requester' for the service, or 'provider' to the service, what else would be required that is specific to this implementation of the service? What additional assets, events, information-flows and decisions would be required in each transaction? What constraints - if any - would the implementation itself impose on transactions? In what ways - for example, response-times, service-volumes, service-quality guarantees - would the content for a service-level agreement for each interface need to be amended specific to this implementation?

- In what business-processes is this implementation used? By what specific means is the use of the implementation *coordinated* or choreographed with other services to deliver the results of each business-process?
- In what ways would the management of this implementation vary from that for the overall abstract-service? What additional *control-information* and *performance-metrics* would be required for this implementation? In what ways does this implementation ensure that the common control-information and performance-metrics are appropriately supported?
- What additional factors determine *quality* within this implementation? How would such quality - including all the shared quality-parameters for the abstract-service - be monitored and maintained within this implementation?

Finally, viewed as a set:

- What are the *trade-offs* between each implementation? In what contexts would one implementation be preferable - more effective - than others, and for what reasons?

> Many of the trade-offs, and factors within the trade-offs, are context-dependent, and themselves may force changes elsewhere.
>
> In some disaster-recovery scenarios, for example, a manual implementation of the service may be essential, because the IT is out of action or no longer exists. The details of the service-level agreement (SLA) will need to change, such as response-time or volume of transactions that can be handled in a given period, but as far as practicable the *parameters* of the SLA should remain the same. Another complication there is that the *asset-type* of some assets in the transaction may also need to change: in that disaster-recovery scenario, the 'pure' virtual asset-type managed by IT would not be available, because the IT is unavailable – hence information will need to arrive as a composite, bundled with a physical-asset such as a paper form, or relational-asset, as in a person-to-person message.
>
> Conversely, changing the main implementation-mechanism may force other competency-changes elsewhere. Converting from a paper form to a machine-readable punch-card or OCR-scan input would speed up the processing, but requires someone to pre-interpret the information into a format that the machine or IT can handle. In a human-only implementation, it's possible to work with low-competency input – just ask the Post Office how to handle badly-scrawled hand-written addresses! – but in a machine-implementation the required 'intelligence' must be moved elsewhere in the process-chain – "please mark the boxes in black ink only", and so on. The *overall* competencies required by the service don't change, but they can be moved around a bit as required in different implementations.

Document the results as described above for abstract-services.

On completion of both assessments – abstract-services and real-services – use gap-analysis and so on to derive requirements for change-projects, as per the standard architecture-cycle.

Compliance and quality

The *purpose* of this section is to identify and assist in implementing methods and metrics to 'real-ise' the enterprise values in every part of everyday practice.

> In this section the emphasis is on expanding outward from the values and principles, identifying and implementing the pervasive-services needed to embed each value in the details of practice. Later on (see p.137) we'll also go the opposite way, working back from the existing quality-management and the like up to the core values and principles that they imply.

For *people*, you'll need to work closely with the practitioners and 'evangelists' for the respective value or principle-set. Beyond those, it's mainly routine business-analysis, so anyone in the architecture team should already have most of the needed skills; but since you could be looking at anything from metrics to procedure-development to details of work-practices, expect to call on or co-opt onto the team any number of subject-matter experts at any level as appropriate.

For *planning*, you'll need to make extensive use of the links in the architecture repository, and also any support you can find for gap-analysis, because much of the work will be about looking for what *isn't* there.

> The anchor-point for all of this is the set of values and principles that you identified right at the start of the architecture (see p.33): it might be useful to go back and review that before starting work here.

The *practice* would be similar to what we've seen already with strategy and innovation (see p.99): the main difference is that it'll be driven mainly from the values and principles already identified in the row-0 'Universals' section of the framework, rather than from a description of new strategy or legislation.

The *performance* here would again often be hard to measure in direct terms, since the main impact is on the effectiveness of the whole. One visible result would be achievement of a compliance certification, because those assessment-processes follow much the same principles as described here – or more precisely, this section identifies the kind of work that needs to done prior to applying for certification. Typical artefacts would be process-models and value-models, and, in conjunction with the 'evangelists', detailed work-instructions and requirements-tests to implement the value-principles in practice.

From value to quality

The key point here is the distinction between function and quality. In standard business-analysis, the requirements are split into two categories: 'functional', and 'non-functional'. But the latter term is misleading, because it implies that these requirements have no function, and therefore don't matter - which is certainly *not* the case. The 'non-functional' requirements are about *quality*, in all its different forms - which brings us back to the enterprise values and principles, because it's in those that the meaning of 'quality' is defined for the enterprise.

Every value and principle implies a *quality-system* through which to implement it in practice. Of these, probably the best-known quality-system is the Deming or Shewhart 'Plan, Do, Check, Act' cycle, with which the US Army's After Action Review (see p.27) aligns exactly, though half a step onward in each case:

- *Plan*: precursor to "What was supposed to happen?"
- *Do*: precursor to "What actually happened?"
- *Check*: precursor to "What was the source of each difference?"
- *Act*: precursor to "What can we learn from this, to do differently next time?"

From the perspective of embedding values and principles into the everyday quality-management, it's simplest if we again rotate the cycle round a bit more:

- *Develop awareness* of the principle (aligns to 'Act')
- *Develop capability* to enact the principle (aligns to 'Plan')
- *Enact* the requirements of the principle (aligns to 'Do')
- *Verify* compliance to the principle (aligns to 'Check')

Since the values need to permeate throughout the enterprise, these 'pervasive-services' need to touch *everywhere*. The responsibility for making this happen will lie with the respective 'evangelists', but as architects we're responsible for embedding appropriate support for it throughout the architecture.

> Bear in mind that there's an impossibly huge scope here: by definition, it covers *every* aspect of the entire enterprise, many times over – at

least once for each core-value, in fact, and often more, where multiple distinct principles devolve from a value. So don't worry about it: there's no way you're going to be able to do this all in one go. To be honest, if you manage to tackle more than a tiny fraction of it in one go, you'll be doing well…

In practice, pick on one value at a time – which also specifies the 'evangelists' with whom you need to work. Decide from there whether you're going to go broad or deep – follow the trails across at a specific framework-layer, or all the way down from root-value to operations – because there won't be enough time to do anything useful if you try to do both at once. If the start-point is a compliance-exercise – ISO-14000 series on environment, for example, or ISO-27000 series on security – then you're almost forced to go deep, but you can perhaps also cover the breadth by running assessments in parallel. The 'best' way is whatever works well in your own context: you'll cover it all eventually, anyway, but just not all at once!

The easiest way to do this is to work your way down through the layers of the Function Model (see p.49). By now this should have been developed to a full tier-3 everywhere; this also gives you a chance to identify all the tier-4 functions in the respective areas, and perhaps more detail than that if required. A 'broad' view would cover all of the functions at a specific tier; a 'deep' view - perhaps more common in practice - would pick a single higher-tier function, and then devolve downward through its 'child'-functions in the next tier, then the 'children' of each of those, and so on.

The 'enact' part of the principle would be embedded within the work of the function itself; the others would each need their own distinct functions and services. Often they might be implemented by the same team, but in some cases - such as financial audit - they may need to be kept separate, either by custom or by law.

Pervasive-services

Identify the value, principle or compliance-requirement to be promulgated throughout the enterprise, and the start-point (initial function on the Function Model). Then:

- How does this principle apply in the context of this function?
- What actions need to be taken within the function to enact this principle?
- What metrics would be needed to monitor and report on the application of this principle within the function?
- What needs to be done to ensure ongoing and increasing *awareness* of the relevance and application of this principle

within the development, management and operation of this function? What business-services would be required in order to support those needs? What capabilities and competencies would be required in those business-services? With what assets, at what locations, in response to what events, and in accordance with what business-rules?

- What needs to be done to ensure ongoing and increasing *capability* to apply the principle within the development, management and operation of this function? What business-services would be required in order to support those needs? What capabilities and competencies would be required in those business-services? With what assets, at what locations, in response to what events, and in accordance with what business-rules?
- What needs to be done to *verify* and audit the application of this principle within the development, management and operation of this function? What business-services would be required in order to support those needs? What capabilities and competencies would be required in those business-services? With what assets, at what locations, in response to what events, and in accordance with what business-rules?

On completion of the assessment for this function, select the next function to be assessed:

- *'broad' assessment*: choose the next 'sibling' function at the same tier, and move down a level when all functions at this tier have been assessed
- *'deep' assessment*: choose the first available 'child' function at the next tier, and continue down the tiers until all functions on this thread have been assessed; then move back up to the starting-level and work downward again for each unassessed function

Loop back to ask the same set of questions with this function. Repeat until all functions in scope have been assessed.

Document the results as links and dependencies in the architecture repository, together with any requirements, risks and the like in the appropriate registers. Dependent on the advice of the respective 'evangelists', you may need to develop one or more Request for Architecture Work documents to initiate a full architecture cycle for structural change.

Resources

- 🕮 Architecture development method and framework: see Tom Graves, *Bridging the Silos: enterprise architecture for IT-architects* (Tetradian, 2008)
- TOGAF (The Open Group Architecture Framework): see www.opengroup.org/architecture/togaf9-doc/arch/
- Association of Professional Futurists: see www.profuturists.org
- Model-driven architecture: see www.omg.org/mda and Wikipedia summary at en.wikipedia.org/wiki/Model-driven_architecture
- Plan / Do / Check / Act quality-cycle: see Wikipedia summary at en.wikipedia.org/wiki/PDCA
- 🕮 Service-architecture and pervasive-services: see Tom Graves, *The Service-Oriented Enterprise: enterprise architecture and viable services* (Tetradian, 2009)

STEP 4: WORK WITH THE REAL WORLD

At this point we have an enterprise architecture that is still somewhat abstract, but is well-enough defined to describe how to change and adapt the real structures of the enterprise to align with high-level changes in strategy, in law and the like. We *know* we can do that now: we've proven it, many times over, in many different ways - and we've proven the value of it, too.

We can optimise horizontally across domains; we can implement strategy top-down. So now it's time to add the ability to go in the opposite direction: manage the same structures from the bottom-up, dealing with the detailed messiness of the real world.

> By the time we've finished, the architecture itself should be able to respond in real-time to the confusions and crises of real-world operations. That's the ideal, anyway: to do it fully requires serious investment in technology and the like, to provide the necessary real-time monitoring to underpin those processes. This wouldn't be necessary or even desirable in many cases, but it's certainly important to watch out for business-critical domains for which that kind of detail would be worthwhile – and the principle is also applicable anywhere.

Purpose and strategy: The focus here is on '***bottom-up***' themes such as business-continuity planning, failure analysis and risk-management, assessing the impact of constraints from the real world on enterprise projects and plans.

> To do this with TOGAF, you have to switch the standard assessment-phases the other way round: 'Technology Architecture' becomes Phase B, and 'Business Architecture' becomes Phase D. It's messy, and it only works for IT, which may be too narrow a scope to be useful in real-world practice, but it does work. Sort-of, anyway.

People and governance: The core team will remain much the same as before - a small group of experienced, innovative generalists - but the others co-opted onto the team for this work will tend to be less the domain-architects, and more the people from front-line support - quality-practitioners, disaster-recovery analysts and so on. Those people will also be generalists, but often more from an engineering bent - some of them literally recruited from the shop floor.

Key attributes for such people would include an inquiring mind, an ability to 'think sideways' – looking at issues from a broader range of practical perspectives – and, preferably, also an ability to 'think with the hands', with literal hands-on experience of the many, many different ways in which things 'go wrong'!

Much of what happens within this stage will, of necessity, be emergent, experimental and unpredictable - and hence will need forms of governance and measurement to match. An Agile style of governance would need to apply where the work is emergent and experimental - though that already aligns well with the modified architecture-development cycle we're using here (see p.20). A conventional escalation-style governance would fit best for real-time responses that cannot be predicted beforehand.

Planning and frameworks: Almost all of this work will depend on the richness and depth of the cross-links in the architecture framework and architecture-repository. Some (see p.130) would ideally also cross-link into a real-time CMDB (configuration-management database) or its equivalent, as the operations-level root for trails of interdependencies and impacts. One probable output of the work would be some kind of executive 'dashboard' - again, ideally to be updated in real-time. Expect also to be creating many models of 'what-if' scenarios.

Practice and methods: All of the work should follow the standard Agile-style architecture-cycle. In some cases - such as with sets of experiments for business-continuity and disaster-recovery planning - the work will need to be governed as cycles-within-cycles, each experiment as a cycle of assessment, design, implementation and lessons-learned review, where the experiments themselves form part of the overall assessment-phases of the larger cycle.

Performance, end-products and metrics: The main metrics here will be around themes such as speed of response and customer-satisfaction. Beyond that, much of the value of this work will be difficult to measure in direct terms: by definition, almost all work on planning for business-continuity and disaster-recovery, for example, is about trying to *prevent* something from happening but being ready for it if it does. And the value of a set of experiments for load-balancing or for business-continuity or the like should only ever be measured in terms of the set *as a whole*: in that kind of emergent context, no one experiment is ever a 'success' or 'failure' on its own, because each is a necessary part of the overall development for the issue in scope.

Designing for service flexibility

The *purpose* of this section is to enhance the flexibility, adaptability, resilience and overall value of service-provision.

> This will depend on and extend the previous work on service-design and service-implementations (see p.110). The more work you've done there, the more value you'll be able to gain here, so you may well find yourself needing to revisit some of that work during this section.

For *people*, you will need to co-opt service-designers, process-managers and process-designers, and people such as quality-management teams who have hands-on experience of dealing with the subtle, near-infinite complexities - and, bluntly, chaos - of real-world service-delivery.

The *planning* will draw extensively on the cross-links in the architecture models and repository, and on end-to-end process models that will usually be held by Operations teams.

The *practice* would use the standard architecture-cycle, usually with straightforward analysis and assessment rather than extensive experimentation. The work will often lead to a need for change-projects, as in Phases E to G of the standard cycle.

The *performance* should be measured in terms of enhanced overall *effectiveness* for the respective services and service-delivery.

Design for escalation

In the real world, things go wrong; things happen that we haven't allowed for in the usual execution of a process. When we're first learning process-design, probably all we'll think about is the standard straight-through process, how 'things ought to go'; but as we gain experience - usually the hard way! - we'll add many more traps for 'exceptions', or what we might call the 'expected unexpected'.

> In BASIC or most other first-level programming languages, a classic "Hello World!" program is usually just one line of code; but by the time its equivalent is usable in a real application, it'll be several hundred lines at least, and in a mission-critical system it might well have grown to several thousand. Designing properly for real-world complexity is not trivial – and it *matters*.

An exception usually calls for some kind of *escalation* - which in practice means shifting the task over to a different set of skills and competencies. Externally it's still the same function, and the same nominal business-service; but internally it calls on another service

– a different *implementation,* using different *capability* – to resolve the need.

Following on from the previous work on services, it should be evident that the escalation will need to respond and report as if it's the same service – even though in fact it's a different service. The escalation itself is relatively simple in terms of its place in the service-choreography – it's an 'upwards' or 'sideways' move that should automatically return back to the original calling service; but the reporting can be quite a bit harder, because the called service will need not only to report in its own right but may also need to mimic the metrics for the calling service.

Another complication is that the escalation may need another *type* of implementation. This typically occurs, for example, when an IT-based process reaches the limits of its analytic competence, and has to hand over to a skilled human operator for guidelines or principles on how to complete the task.

> One everyday example of this occurs in mail-sorting. These days, most mail is sorted by machines, many of them with very sophisticated capabilities to read and decipher even hand-written addresses. But when the machine can't cope with some horrible mis-spelt scrawl, it spits the letter out into a queue for manual interpretation – because humans can handle that kind of mess much better than machines can. And if the routine operator can't handle it, it gets escalated to the Dead Letter Office – the *real* interpretation experts. Given the quality – or lack of it – of many people's handwriting, it's a surprisingly small percentage of the post that ends up on the 'undeliverable mail' pile: a real tribute to the way the *overall* mail-sorting service works.
>
> If there *isn't* an appropriate escalation-mechanism in place for each function – including a 'none of the above' service that has ultimate responsibility for the unexpected – then things can get into a *serious* mess, very quickly indeed. One of our government clients discovered this the hard way, when they faced a huge outcry in the press about 'fundamental failures' that turned out in practice to be a trivial data-design error – specifically, a key-field requiring date of birth in a 'Person' record for an as-yet unborn child. The problem was that they had no manual mechanism or override to resolve that 'unlikely' yet all too real possibility – so it sat there for some months, quietly festering in the Too Hard basket, until some over-eager journalist spotted it in the performance-metrics on the department's own website, and interpreted it the wrong way. The results were extremely unpleasant, and acutely embarrassing for all concerned: you have been warned!

The service of escalation

For each service in scope:

- What exceptions does the service handle within itself, without needing external escalation? How are these 'in-scope' escalations recorded within the service's reporting-metrics?
- What mechanisms does the service have, to identify exceptions that are beyond its competence? To what other services, and how, does it notify this non-competence? What escalation-mechanisms does the service have, to pass these exceptions to other services? How are these 'out-of-scope' escalations recorded within the service's reporting-metrics?
- What competences are required to handle these 'out-of-scope' escalations? What would these require within the services that handle those escalations? How would these escalations be recorded in the called service's reporting-metrics? Given that the called service may handle escalations from multiple calling services, how are these distinctions recorded in the reporting-metrics?
- Via what transactions would the 'out of-scope' escalation be passed to the other service? What would need to be returned to the calling service to signal successful resolution or non-resolution of the escalation? What else would need to be returned to the calling service?
- What happens if the called service itself does not have the competencies to resolve the escalation? If further escalated to another service, what needs to be done to ensure that the trail of escalations and returns is maintained intact? What audit-information is required in order to verify that some kind of closure is achieved in each case?
- What capabilities, competencies and skillsets would be required to resolve a 'none of the above' escalation in this context? Are these competencies available within the enterprise? If so, how are they available, and by what means would they be accessed? If not, or if there is no possible resolution, how is this notified to the original service-requestor?

Document the results as models and cross-connections in the architecture-repository, and risks and requirements in their respective registers. In conjunction with the process-designers and service-analysts, outline a Request for Architecture Work for each significant set of risks and requirements, to lead to change-projects as appropriate.

Design for resilience

Another aspect of service-management is load-balancing - which we could think of as a kind of 'sideways escalation', because much the same principles are involved.

This draws directly from the trade-off analysis we did we did in looking at services in the previous stage (see p.111). There, we were aiming to identify the 'best' or optimal implementation for a given set of circumstances. Here, we do much the same, but we design with the awareness that *the circumstances can change* - often changing in real-time, too. So what we need is a *set* of implementations, so that we can switch between them - or switch them on and off, so to speak - as the circumstances change.

> In the IT industry, this is the principle behind 'virtualisation', server-sharing and similar load-balancing techniques. But a simpler example would, again, be in sorting the mail. The bulk of the mail is handled by the big sorting-machines in the major mail-centres; but in the smaller sorting-offices, and even in parts of the main ones, some of the mail will be sorted by hand. An increasing amount of mail is pre-sorted by IT instead: it comes in as an electronic file of gas-bills, for example, and goes out as neatly-sealed envelopes complete with the bar-code for the address. If the IT breaks down, the envelopes switch over into the standard machine-sort; if a machine breaks down; the sorting-office switches over to manual sort, with multiple streams running in parallel – it's slower per stream, and it's more expensive overall, but it works, and the mail still goes out on time. In the Christmas rush, when millions of scrawled hand-addressed greeting-cards hit the mail-boxes, the sorting office calls in temporary staff to take on the load, keeping the ordinary mail flowing through the machines in the usual way. Balancing the load, whichever way it comes: that's what it's all about in sorting the mail.

To do this, we need to go back to the abstract-service again, this time paying as much attention to the service-choreography as to the services themselves - because it would be the choreography's responsibility to monitor the context and handle the switching between service-implementations, in order to control the actual balancing of service-load. The service-choreography is itself a service, so we can use much the same assessment approach there as for the main services.

The services balancing-act

For each abstract-service in scope:

- Where does this abstract-service fit within which end-to-end business-processes? What services drive and govern service-choreography for these business-processes?
- What implementations are available for this abstract-service? What are the trade-offs and design-decisions between them? In what ways do the required or available capabilities and competencies differ between the implementations? What is the availability of each required capability and competence within the respective business unit? In what ways would such availability act as a constraint on the viable performance throughput and quality for each implementation?
- What are the typical conditions under which each implementation would be the optimal or preferred version? Under which conditions would the implementation be less optimal but still acceptable, and why? Under what conditions, and why, should a specific implementation *not* be used? And how would the service-choreography recognise the respective conditions and switch between implementations accordingly?
- Is it possible to run multiple instances of the implementation in parallel, to increase overall throughput? If so, in what ways would the service-choreography need to change, to manage this? What opportunities, risks or issues arise from such parallel operation?
- Is it possible to run multiple types of implementations in parallel, to increase overall throughput? If so, in what ways would the service-choreography need to change, to manage this? What opportunities, risks or issues arise from such parallel operation? What requirements would this imply for each implementation, and for the service-choreography?
- What impact would implementation-switching and parallel-operation have on the service-level agreements for the abstract service? What performance-metrics would be required to monitor and manage this?
- What impacts would implementation-switching and parallel-operation have on the end-to-end processes? For example, will switching cause bottlenecks in the process-flow on either side of the abstract-service, or elsewhere in the end-to-end process? How will such whole-of-system impacts be identified, monitored and managed?

Document the results as models and cross-connections in the architecture-repository, and risks and requirements in their respective registers. As before, work with the process-designers and service-analysts to outline a Request for Architecture Work for each significant set of risks and requirements, to lead to change-projects as appropriate.

Planning for business-continuity

The ***purpose*** of this section is to identify the potential or actual impacts of a given system-failure or system-change scenario, and suggest, design or implement appropriate means to resolve or mitigate that impact.

For the ***people***, you'll again need to co-opt from the service-designers, process-designers, quality-teams and risk-managers. Who you'll want most of all, though, are 'the old hands' who've dealt with all manner of real-world chaos, and have the bloody-minded cynicism, pessimism, tenacity and destructive inventiveness of the experienced senior tester.

> Not just the 'old hands', of course: the inquisitive, unaware, unthinking anarchy of the 'young hands' is often a lot 'worse' – which makes them even better for finding out the real risks in any system. Young males are often the best of all for this: set up a suitable simulation safely away from the real production area, let a gang of 'tween-agers' loose on it, then sit back and watch how quickly things fall apart – you'll soon have plenty to test and repair!

The ***planning*** will again draw extensively on the cross-links in the architecture models and repository, and on end-to-end process models that will usually be held by Operations teams.

> Much of this will depend on and draw from the previous work on design for system resilience and flexibility (see p.125). In many cases, the work within a maturity-stage can be done in any order, but this isn't one of them: you *will* need to have done at least some of that work on resilience before you tackle this.

The ***practice*** would use the standard architecture-cycle, this time usually with extensive back-and-forth between experiment and analysis for risk-assessment. As in the previous section, the work will often lead to a need for change-projects, as in Phases E to G of the standard cycle; to support real-time impact-analysis, these change-projects might include manual or automated processes to use the cross-links in the architecture-repository to warn risk-managers and others of the effective performance-impacts of any potential or actual failures.

Once again, measurement of ***performance*** will be difficult here, because the whole point of much of the work is to prevent things happening, and hence much of 'success' measurable only in terms of what *doesn't* happen. So the main metrics will again be around customer-satisfaction, speed of response and the like. Typical outcomes would include models of failure-and-response scenarios, failure-impact maps, and - co-developed with risk-managers - procedures and work-instructions for 'safe-fail' risk-mitigation and risk-recovery activities.

The impact of disaster

Business-continuity and disaster-recovery planning provide some of the greatest challenges to the architecture, literally testing it to destruction if we don't pay attention to what it shows us. Yet that process itself will show us not only how to make the architecture more robust, but also how to *use* the architecture to guide failure-response: we can fight against it in futility, or learn to work *with* it, to everyone's benefit.

Strategy and other top-down plans provide an idealised picture of how we want our world to be; constraints coming bottom-up from the operations space tell us what the world really is. Somewhere in the middle, the two forces meet - and often clash, sometimes with ugly consequences for the architecture and the enterprise. Despite all our nice plans, the real world is *messy* - and it always will be, whether we like it or not. No matter what the company rule-books may say, the only *real* law is Murphy's: and Murphy rules supreme…

> Taking a slightly twisted view on this, Murphy is not architecture's enemy, but one of the best friends we could have!
>
> The essential word in Murphy's Law is the one that's most often missed out: "If something can go wrong, it *probably* will". The key to Murphy is *uncertainty* – and if we skip the 'probably', we miss that vital clue. So if Murphy *is* a law – and hard-edged science and hard-earned experience alike would suggest not only that it is a law, but the only real law that there is – then it has to apply to everything, *including itself*. In which case, if Murphy's Law can go wrong, it probably will: hence most of the time, things work as expected – which is why we get the illusion that things are predictable. Just not predictable *all* of the time…
>
> But there's another twist yet, because what Murphy also shows us is that things *can* go right, if we let them. And if we only let things go right in expected ways, we're limiting our chances!

> Always remember that risk and opportunity are the flipsides of each other: every opportunity is a risk, and every risk an opportunity. If you build that awareness into your architecture, you've already built in a key component for your support of business-continuity and disaster-recovery planning.

For this part of the work, though, all we need to know is what *else* happens when something happens - something 'goes wrong', something unexpected, something 'out of the ordinary'. In other words, to trace the *impact* of an unexpected, unplanned-for event.

We always do this bottom-up, because the row-6 Operations layer is actually the only place where 'the enterprise' touches the real world. Ideas may begin at the top, but reality exists at the bottom. So in a typical impact-analysis scenario, we imagine that some critical component has suddenly disappeared: there's been a fire, a flood, a break-in, a simple breakdown; you've just lost a server, a submarine cable, a sorting-depot. What happens? What can you not now do if that's gone? What *else* won't work? Whose performance figures will be hit, and by how much? How long - if at all - can we keep going without that item?

> We also need to ask what kind of workarounds are available, how long we can keep going on those, how to recover afterwards, and so on – but that comes a little later, as we'll see in the next section (see p.134). For now we're only concerned with tracing the impact of the event.

Enterprise architecture comes into this picture in that the architecture repository will by now hold a vast amount of information about what connects with what, and the nature and bindedness of each of those cross-dependencies. This makes impact analysis almost *easy* - in fact some toolsets will do much of the modelling automatically, at not much more than the click of a mouse. All we need do is follow the trails, and watch the impacts ripple upward through the entire enterprise.

> The ideal, of course, is to be able not only to do this beforehand, so to speak, in imaginary failure-scenarios, but to do it in real-time too, to see instantly the probable effect of an actual failure, to prioritise responses and issue alerts, all the way up to the executive if necessary.
>
> This is no pipe-dream: some enterprise-architecture toolsets already provide interfaces to configuration-management databases, and some CMDBs in turn receive feeds from real-time alerts – so it *is* all doable, even now. What it *isn't* is either simple or cheap: to be more accurate, it's fiendishly complex and ruinously expensive to set up, and probably uncomfortably fragile once it's running. Might be worth it for the really mission-critical systems, though. But before you try to jump in with the

real-time stuff, you'll need to get the impact analysis working with ordinary offline scenarios – and that's what we tackle here.

Impact from the bottom up

Working with risk-managers, define a scenario in which one or more key items have been put either temporarily or permanently out of service. Identify the items in the architecture repository, first defining appropriate entries for them if required. Then ask:

- To what is this item connected? At this level [initially, the row-6 Operations layer], what assets, functions, locations, capabilities, events, business-decisions and their composites depend on this item? What is the business-criticality of each dependency?
- If an 'owner'-responsibility relationship exists for the item, how will the 'owner' be notified of the failure? What decisions and actions will the 'owner' need to take? On what would such decisions and actions depend?
- What 'owner'-responsibilities can be identified for dependent items connected to the failed item? How will those 'owners' be notified, what actions and decisions will they need to take, and on what will those depend in turn?
- What resource-allocations and performance-metrics will be affected by the failure of this item?
- Overall, what is the business-criticality of this item? What overall impact will it have on business-critical metrics, and on any or all of the enterprise 'pervasives'? In what way does the criticality change over time - for example, survivable for one minute, one hour, one day, one week?
- What impact will the failure have on the next level up [initially, the row-5 'Implement' operations-planning layer]? What are the assets, functions, locations, capabilities, events, business-decisions and their composites that will be affected? What dependencies exist from these affected items for items on the next layer down, and so on downward to actual operations? What else will be affected, and what will their knock-on impacts be, as the effects ripple up and down again to the operations layer?

The last set of questions move up a layer; use this to recurse through the questions from the start, moving up another layer at each pass, until impacts can be assessed right the way up to the row-0 'Universals'.

Document any newly-identified items and dependencies in the architecture repository, together with any further risks, opportunities and issues. Working with risk-managers and others, identify requirements for change-projects to mitigate these risks.

The role of the architect here is solely to provide decision-support: all design-decisions and suchlike would be the responsibility of risk-managers and operations specialists.

The impact dashboard

Following from the previous impact-analyses, assess what information will be needed at various levels of the enterprise in order to respond appropriately to incidents of varying severity:

- What categories of incidents have significant impacts for the operation and viability of the enterprise? In what ways would you prioritise incidents, for which stakeholders, and why?
- For each category of incident, what information do the stakeholders need in order to resolve or mitigate the incident impact? In what timespan would this information be needed, and from which sources would or could it be derived? What transforms would be needed to present this information appropriately and meaningfully for the respective audience?

Document the requisite metrics and transforms, and their dependencies on the respective assets, functions and the like, in the architecture repository, with any identified risks, opportunities and issues in their respective registers. If appropriate, work with system-designers and others, outline requirements for design and implementation of a suitable 'impact dashboard'.

Fail-safe and safe-fail

That work on impact-analysis and impact trails provides us with an effective list of failure-priorities. Some of the potential failures would be almost trivial, or the respective workarounds fairly self-evident; but some are most definitely not, and we need to design appropriate ways around them. Here we need to contrast two different approaches:

- *fail-safe*: no viable alternative – must not fail, because if it does, there is no direct possibility of recovery
- *safe-fail*: is allowed to fail 'gracefully', with fallback to lower-grade alternatives

Fail-safe is the obvious preference, but courtesy of Murphy's Law, it's never actually achievable in practice. The best we can do is deal with the consequences of each failure, and make every effort to learn from those consequences, to extend ever closer towards the 'fail-safe' ideal.

> In some cases the consequences of the failure of a 'fail-safe' could well be that someone dies – so this isn't a trivial matter. 'Lessons-learned' is an essential part of any quality-system, which is why the architecture-cycle has that explicit 'lessons-learned' phase at the end of the cycle. Often there will be a lot of pressures to skip over that 'lessons-learned' analysis and go straight into the next piece of architecture assessment, but it's essential that you take the time to stop, think, reflect, learn – because if you don't, you're literally putting lives and livelihoods at risk. Don't skip it: lessons-learned *matters*.

The aim in safe-fail is that we aim *always* to have alternatives of some kind. One option is to use multiple-redundancy in system-design. Aircraft navigation-systems, for example, will use two or more systems in parallel, of different vintages and with different technologies, ultimately right back to sextant and compass - so if one system fails, we fall back 'gracefully' to the next in line, and we can compare between them in case of doubt.

> Another alternative is that we may set up circumstances in which failure doesn't matter – such as in a carefully-isolated 'practice field' in which people can test out those parts of skills in which learning only takes place by making mistakes.

This is why the principle of abstract-services versus service-implementations (see p.110) is so important, because it allows us to switch between different implementations without changing the fundamental interface. The *values* in parameters to the service level agreement might change - for example, the transaction-volume may drop, or the response-time increase - but the SLA parameters should remain unchanged; the *details* of the interface may change - for example, if the IT-system fails, we may have to drop back to using paper-based forms, or even just word-of-mouth - but as far as practicable, the content and *structure* of the interface should remain the same.

In essence, it's the same principles as in load-balancing (see p.128): by keeping the interfaces the same, we shift the complexity to the service-choreography. And that's much simpler to manage - it's already designed for this kind of service-switching, because that's how it handles the existing end-to-end business-processes.

> To take this to an extreme, a risk-management colleague working in the banking sector asks executives to imagine that their bank-branch has suddenly ceased to exist: it's burned down, hit by an earthquake,

> or simply that the power-supply has been cut because the electricity-substation has failed – the reason *why* doesn't much matter here. The next question: what is the very first department they need to get going again? Answer: *the mail-room* – because communication, even in simple note-form, is the key to coordination. IT is important, yes, but it takes *time* to set up – and time is at an absolute premium in any emergency.

So to design for fail-safe and safe-fail - to *design* for failure - we need to re-assess the abstract-services and the implementations, and the service-choreography that links them together.

Design for failure

For each priority failure-scenario:

- What are the abstract-services in context for this failure-scenario? What are the transactions, resource-requirements, service-level agreement templates and reporting-metrics for each?
- What implementations exist for each abstract-service? What are the characteristics and trade-offs for each? What specific amendments do they each require for the transactions, resource-requirements, service-level agreement templates and reporting-metrics?
- What are the fallbacks and failure-characteristics for each failure-scenario in which each abstract-service and its implementations are in context? Does the scenario require a fail-safe or safe-fail fallback-response? What transition-management would be required in service-choreography to switch between implementations in a fallback scenario? What additional requirements - if any - will be placed on the service-choreography to satisfy the fallback needs?
- Are all fallback requirements for an abstract-service covered by the existing implementations? If not, what amendments or additional implementations would be required?

Document any newly-identified items and dependencies in the architecture repository, together with any further risks, opportunities and issues. Working with risk-managers and others, identify requirements for change-projects to improve fail-safe and safe-fail handling for failure incidents.

As before, the architect is there solely to provide decision-support for system design: all design-decisions and suchlike would be the responsibility of risk-managers and operations specialists.

From qualities to values

The *purpose* of this section is to verify the links between the pervasive-services that promulgate the enterprise values, and the quality-systems and support-services that are already in action in the Operations context.

> In effect, this is the bottom-up version of the top-down work on compliance and quality that we did in the previous step (see p.117). What this is really about is completing the chains of relationships for the enterprise 'pervasives', and making amendments such that the chains are firmly anchored at each end.
>
> Once again, the overall scope is impossibly huge: you'll probably *never* cover all of it, let alone cover it all in one go. Instead, pick on a 'theme' that is already important to the business – security, perhaps, or compliance to some specific new regulation – and use that as a 'trawl-net' to see what comes up. *Always* link it back to a specific business concern and specific business value: for anything else, take a quick yet comprehensive note of what you've found, park the note somewhere such that you know you can find it again – such as in a 'for review' section of the architecture repository – and toss it back into the maelstrom of everyday activity, so that you can fish it out again later when the right opportunity comes around.

For *people*, you'll need to co-opt much the same grizzled crew as before: risk-managers, quality-managers, process-managers and suchlike - people who work with the detail and deep realities of operational quality, security, safety and so on.

As before, the *planning* will draw extensively on the cross-links in the architecture repository, and on the models developed in the earlier work on compliance and quality. Other key information-sources include operational procedures and work-instructions on quality-management and the like, and, perhaps even more, the personal experience of the operations practice-specialists.

For governance, the *practice* should follow the standard architecture cycle, though again this is likely to follow an iterative or recursive pattern. Although some of this work will necessarily be exploratory, each cycle or set of cycles should have a defined business-purpose, with defined business-outcomes.

The *performance* would be measured in part by the usual metrics such as customer-satisfaction and response-time, and in part also by broader impacts on overall service-quality and compliance to the enterprise 'pervasives'.

Quality in practice

So far, much of the discussion about values and qualities has been focussed at the top – the problem of POSIWID and so on. Yet the place where most of the crucial quality-issues and quality-actions occur is right at the other end of the scale, down in the detail of service-delivery. And there are plenty of people who already work on quality – and qualities – in that space: what we need to do now is connect up with them, and create links to them and for them in our architecture.

So this is the corollary to the work we did on quality in the previous step. Here we need to explore operations-level quality-management, and use that to identify and verify the implied values and support for those values, all the way back up the 'pervasives'-trees.

The simplest way to do this is a simple subtraction: if it's not delivering something (a delivery-service), reporting on something or managing something (links to a management-service, or those services themselves) or coordinating something in an end-to-end process (coordinating-service), it's probably about quality of some kind – either managing the quality itself, or enhancing capability to support that quality. If that's the case, we need to anchor it to the respective 'pervasive' – or identify and model the implied 'pervasive' if we haven't done so already.

Connecting to quality

For each activity at the operations-level that is not directly related to service-delivery, management or process-execution:

- What does the activity *do*? What role does it play in the operation and effectiveness of the whole?
- What is the business-value and business-purpose of the work? Who or what determines its purpose and value?
- What qualities – for example, security, safety, privacy, trust, efficiency, reliability, maintenance, waste-minimisation, or any of the other '-ities' or '-ilities' – are enacted or represented in this activity? In what ways and via what means does the activity weave the various qualities together?
- What formal standards – if any – does this activity implement: ITIL or COBIT for IT, for example, or Six Sigma or ISO-900x, or the many ISO and other standards on security, safety, environment-management and the like? How does the activity verify its performance against the respective standard?

- In what ways does this link to business-principles, architecture-principles, design-principles, operational principles and so on? What other guiding-principles are implied in the existence and operation of the activity?
- Who or what does the work of supporting and enacting this quality in practice? What skills, competencies and capabilities do they need in order to do this? If the quality-support is embedded within the functionality of a machine or IT-application, what skills, competencies and capabilities are needed in those who create that functionality, and in those who operate it? By what means would you verify that the required skills and suchlike are not only available but applied in appropriate ways?
- In what ways does this activity link with the enterprise 'pervasives'? What pervasive-services – develop awareness, develop capability, verify and audit – are implied or required to support the qualities in this activity? By what business processes – if any – are the respective pervasive-services linked to the activity, to support and enhance the required quality? Via what means does this link back, all the way up the respective pervasive-services tree, to the 'parent' quality in the enterprise 'Universals'?
- Who is responsible for linking quality in practice to the respective 'pervasives'? What skills, competencies and capabilities are required for such practitioners? How is this work managed and coordinated around the practical concerns of day-to-day service-delivery.
- Are there any aspects of quality in the activity that are *not* currently recorded as enterprise 'pervasives', or anchored to such 'pervasives'? If so, what changes would this imply to the ways in which the 'pervasives' are recorded and portrayed in the architecture-repository, and to the implementation of any or all other 'pervasives'?

Document in the architecture repository any new items, interdependencies and crosslinks, together with any risks, opportunities and issues. Working with quality-managers and others as appropriate, identify requirements for change-projects that might be needed to support quality-management in any of its forms.

Once again, the architect's primary role here is that of decision-support: all design-decisions and suchlike would be the responsibility of quality-managers and operations specialists.

Resources

- 🕮 Whole-of-enterprise architecture: see Tom Graves, *Real Enterprise Architecture: beyond IT to the whole enterprise* (Tetradian, 2008)
- 🕸 TOGAF (The Open Group Architecture Framework): see www.opengroup.org/architecture/togaf9-doc/arch/
- 🕮 Abstract-services and service-implementations: see Tom Graves, *The Service-Oriented Enterprise: enterprise architecture and viable services* (Tetradian, 2009)

STEP 5: POWERING ON

By the end of the previous stage we've expanded our repertoire of assessment-directions almost to the full range: focussed, sideways, top-down, and bottom-up. We have a lot of flexibility there. So to move our architecture from managed, to optimised well enough to tackle some of the more intractable problems and issues, we now need to be able to fit these options together into any required combinations - a style of assessment we could call 'spiral-out', because we move outward in any appropriate direction from the chosen starting-point, until we've explored and understood the context well enough to describe a solution that really *does* work.

> The themes we tackle here include resolution of intractable 'pain-points' or 'wicked problems'; the quest for enhanced effectiveness; and identification and response to new opportunities. These are all of high value to the enterprise, and all notoriously difficult to solve in practice.
>
> Yet although these are some of the most important issues to the business – ones that they would have wanted to us to address straight away, right at the start – note that we *don't* try to tackle them in depth before this stage. There'll have been few hints and tentative steps – and demonstrably useful ones, too – but not much more than that. If we *had* tried to tackle the whole issues head-on before now, we would almost certainly have gotten ourselves into even more of a tangle than that we'd started with – the classic outcome of so many IT-centric 'solutions' to whole-of-business problems. But by this stage, we *do* now have the architecture maturity and cross-enterprise experience that these issues actually demand – so now is our chance to get it right, and deliver on the full promise of enterprise architecture.

Purpose and strategy: The overall purpose here is a stronger integration of the enterprise as a unified whole. The strategic focus will be on issues that must be tackled with an iterative '***spiral-out***' approach: we start at any appropriate point in the framework, and spiral outward from there via successive iterations through the architecture cycle. At the start, in most cases, there will be no clear definition of the probable end-point: only a loose summary of the overall issue and need, and the context for the exploration, from which the required outcome will eventually emerge.

> We're a long way beyond traditional TOGAF territory here: in fact the reflexive IT-centrism behind conventional 'enterprise architecture' is a common *cause* of the problems we'll face in this stage.

Do *not* try to tackle any of these issues until you've fully broken free from the 'IT-only' box. Most of the issues here can only be addressed with a true whole-of-enterprise awareness, assessing all the trade-offs between the different domains and implementations. At the very least, *all* of these issues will include a strong human component, and trying to tackle them with an IT-centric attitude will guarantee that you would only make things worse: you have been warned!

People and governance: The core team would continue largely unchanged from the previous step, but 'temporary members' co-opted for specific projects could now include *anyone*, from literally any part of the enterprise - including 'outsiders', in some cases.

The required skillsets and competencies will vary even more than before, according to needs of the context. The most valuable of these skills, though, will again be the ability to take a generalist view, creating links across the functions and silos of the business.

Governance-models will need to be yet more flexible than before. The core requirement would be that there *is* some consistent form of governance used throughout, with full traceability and transparency of decision-making, and appropriate maintenance and monitoring of results. The real complication is that many project-types here will need a fully emergent approach, requiring many iterations within the one project, often with repeated explorations over the same ground, to arrive at a viable result. The project-sponsors do need to be aware and acknowledge that much of the work will *necessarily* be experimental at times, with no certain guarantees of 'success' other than at the level of the whole.

Planning and frameworks: In addition to the models, structures and other information in the architecture repository, risk-registers and the like, all of this work will depend - in part, at least - on models derived from systems-thinking and the 'living organism' metaphor for the enterprise. Some preparation may be needed to introduce the underlying concepts behind these models to team-members and, eventually, the wider enterprise community.

One of the best sources for this is the series of books produced by Peter Senge and his colleagues at MIT Sloan School of Management, such as *The Fifth Discipline* and *The Dance of Change*. The former book is somewhat hard going but worth the effort, the latter more a 'cook-book' sprinkled with case-studies and practical recipes – but both strongly recommended, anyway.

Practice and methods: As before, all of the work should follow the standard Agile-style architecture-cycle. For experimental work, use the principle of cycles-within-cycles, where each experiment is run under the same governance-cycle within the standard assessment-cycle governance.

Performance, end-products and metrics: By this stage there are no simple metrics for architecture performance: the only meaningful measure is in terms of the success of the whole enterprise. It's still useful - and important - to continue to measure the perception of the value of the architecture unit itself, via the usual metrics such as response-time and customer-satisfaction; but beyond that the unit has much the same role as any other background 'pervasives' team, such as knowledge-management or environmental awareness, and should be monitored and measured accordingly.

The end-products of each architecture-cycle will vary enormously, dependent on the context and need: still plenty of architecture-models and the like, but overall moving steadily closer towards a context in which the architecture is 'owned' by the enterprise at large, with the architecture unit providing background guidance and assistance - 'the architecture is the dialogue', as we'll see more in the next chapter.

The service-oriented enterprise

The ***purpose*** of this section is to explore more deeply the *practical* meaning of 'service' within the enterprise. For here, this takes two key forms: enterprise-scope integration of all the previous work on business-services, and reflection on the practical implications of the *human* meaning of 'service'.

Much of this revolves around the ***people*** side of the enterprise and its architecture - so you'll need to engage a variety of specialists from the HR domains for much of this work, along with process-designers and whole-of-system integrators from anywhere around the enterprise.

For ***planning***, the links *between* entities in the architecture repository will become even more important than before, as they'll highlight the mutual interdependencies between the services of the enterprise. Chief amongst these links are some we've barely begun to address as yet, namely the *people-based* interdependencies of mutual responsibility and mutual service, which underpin the *viability* of the enterprise within its ecosystem. A key part of the preparation here will include developing a deeper awareness of these themes and their impacts on the function, structure and purpose of the enterprise.

The comparisons between the classic 'enterprise as machine' metaphor and the more realistic metaphor of 'enterprise as living organism', together with the core systems-thinking concepts and models for the service-oriented enterprise, are explored in more depth in the book *The Service Oriented Enterprise.*

During this section we'll also need to tackle more of the human aspects of the enterprise – the themes on which the resolution of almost all intractable 'wicked problems' will depend. Key concepts on this are described in another companion book, *Power and Response-ability: the human side of systems.* One example theme is that whilst the physics definition of power approximates to 'the ability to do work', most social definitions of power are closer to the ability to *avoid* work – a fact with enormous implications for the viability of the enterprise...

Although much of the work here is iterative, each item of ***practice*** should follow the same architecture-cycle as before. It's unlikely that there would be many 'big projects' for the implementation sections of the cycle, though there would be a sizeable amount of ongoing 'project-like' work on service-integration and on keeping track of responsibilities and their ownership by individual people.

The ***performance*** can really only be measured in terms of the enhanced success of the areas of the enterprise that are in focus for each architecture-review. Examples would include improved handovers in end-to-end process flows from a stronger service-orientation, and improved communication - and reduced overall confusion - as a result of an emphasis on responsibility and item-ownership.

Everything is a service

There's been a strong emphasis on services and service-oriented design throughout the architecture development (for example, see p.48, p.110 and p.125); here is where we bring it all together into a single integrated view of the *service-oriented enterprise.*

As we've seen earlier, we can summarise services in terms of four distinct categories:

- *delivery-services*: create and provide the 'deliverables' of the overall service
- *management-services*: guide service-delivery in 'vertical' silos structured around business-function
- *coordination-services*: guide 'horizontal' end-to-end business-processes
- *pervasive-services*: ensure that service-delivery remains 'on purpose'

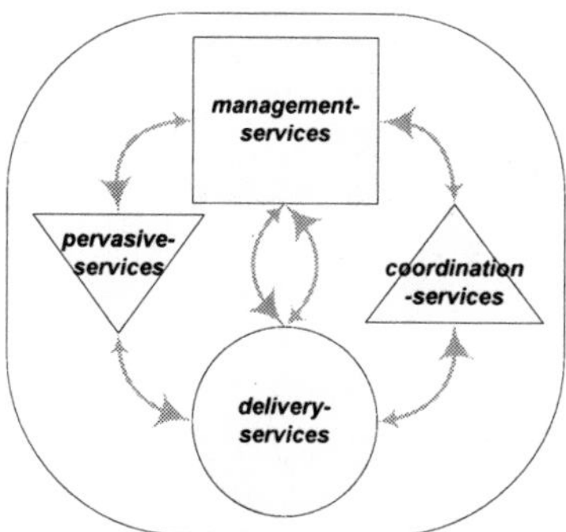

Four categories of services

So far we've viewed these as separate types of services, but there's a further twist we should also take into account here: at a conceptual level, *every service has exactly the same structure*. Services are fractal or recursive in nature: each delivery-service also does its own management, coordination and links to pervasive qualities; each management-service delivers its service of 'management-services', and so on. Every service must include, either directly or indirectly, every other type of service. So we can use that fact as a means to verify 'service-completeness' in any part of the enterprise, and in the enterprise as a whole.

The simplest way to do this is to go back to the Function Model, and start the verification process from there. (Given their nature, and the small size of the respective business-units, it's likely that few of the coordination-services or pervasive-services will show up even at the tier-3 level of the model, so do remember to include them explicitly in this assessment.) We then use an extended version of a framework known as the Viable System Model to check that all the required links are present in some form or other.

In many cases, the required support-services or links will in fact exist, but are not recognised as such: they may be implied in what is done in practice, or be subsumed into 'general responsibilities of line-management'. The catch in such cases is that there may be no explicit means to ensure that the work required for the inter-service link is actually done. In other cases, the links may be erratic, or absent altogether: the symptoms of the disconnect will usually be all too evident, but the cause may not. One common quality-management example is a confusion between 'correction' - "fix it up to get the job out of the door" - versus 'corrective action' - "make sure it doesn't happen again". All of the links need to be fully present and fully working before the service - and, in turn, the enterprise itself - can be said to be 'viable'.

> Note that some – perhaps most – of these questions will have come up already, in some form or another, in earlier parts of architecture-development. What we do here is bring them all together into a single unified review, with more of an emphasis on *integration* of the interdependencies between services.
>
> In practice, the checklist that follows provides a minimum set of tests to apply: add further context-specific tests to the list as appropriate.

Interdependencies of service

Apply the following checklist to each function and service in scope, at each tier of the Function Model:

- *Policy*: What is the service's *purpose*? Who or what defines its *policy*? From where are these policy-services obtained?
- *Strategy*: What is the current *strategy*? In relation to what outside *relationships*? Who defines these? From where are these strategy-services obtained?
- *Manage*: How are the service's *tasks defined, managed* and *monitored*? From where are these services obtained?
- *Verify*: What random checks or *audits* are used to *verify* performance? From where are these services obtained?
- *Coordinate*: How is the service *coordinated* with other services? From where are these coordination-services obtained?
- *Tasks*: What does the service *do*? How does it do it? How does it support its 'child' delivery-services (if any)? From where are these child-services obtained?
- *Exceptions*: How does the service identify, escalate and resolve any *run-time exceptions* ('correction')? From where are these escalation-services obtained?
- *Quality*: What *corrective-action* does the service undertake for *causes* of issues? From where are these services obtained?
- *Track*: How does the service *track* and manage *quality-issues* and other issues? From where are these services obtained?
- *Improve*: How does the service manage *improvement* of its *processes*? From where are these services obtained?
- How are all of these links and interdependencies identified, modelled, managed and maintained?

Each link should reference services that this service 'consumes', either from other services elsewhere in the enterprise, or from subsidiary functions and tasks within itself. In principle, every one of these services must exist *somewhere,* otherwise the organisation would be unable to operate - or operate well, at least.

Document any identified gaps, and resolve these gaps wherever practicable.

Being of service

For this piece we need to take another slight twist on 'service', and review it in human terms: the concept of '*being of service*' to others. This notion is so old that it may seem positively archaic to some, but it actually goes right to the root of 'enterprise': if the enterprise is "a group of people coordinating their efforts toward a common mission", the coordination itself takes place through bonds of mutual service and mutual responsibility.

If everything in the enterprise is a service, not only are all of those services linked together via mutual responsibilities, but each of the assets, functions, locations, capabilities, events, decisions and composites that underpin them implies a responsibility. What this means in practice is that *someone* should be responsible for each and every entity in the architecture framework: a *personal* commitment of responsibility to and with that entity, on behalf of the shared enterprise.

> These commitments, incidentally, are *aspirational assets* – in effect, a declaration by someone that they 'belong' to the entity, and hence to the shared enterprise – 'that which is greater than self' – via that commitment to the entity.
>
> For most architectural purposes, that kind of detail is too arcane to be of much concern. Where it starts to matter is that responsibility – especially in its literal form as 'response-ability' – is closely coupled with 'ability to do work' in any functional sense. When morale is damaged, for example, the aspirational-asset bonds are weakened, and hence 'response-ability' weakened in turn – which means that critical components are mislaid, critical activities are not done (or not done well), and problems proliferate throughout the enterprise: the overall 'ability to do work' goes down like a brick. Conversely, when morale is enhanced, 'response-ability' rises with it – and with that, in turn, the effectiveness of the enterprise. Responsibility *matters.*
>
> Identifying the nature and scale of that aspirational status is the role of the SEMPER diagnostic, as described in the companion book *SEMPER and SCORE: enhancing enterprise effectiveness*; but to assess its impact, which architecture-entities are affected, and where to start to resolve it or leverage from it, you'll need the lists and linkages of responsibilities that we identify here.

Responsibility is the key to the viability, agility and effectiveness of the enterprise. In effect, we need a RACI matrix for each entity in the architecture:

- *responsible* or 'accountable': the business-owner of the entity (there should be exactly one person - not just role, but real person - with this assignment for each entity, at all times)
- *assists*: active stakeholder - those who assist the responsible person in the overall usage or application of the entity (active engagement)
- *consulted*: committed stakeholder - those whose opinions may be sought concerning the entity (two-way communication)
- *informed*: passive stakeholder - those who need to be kept up-to-date on changes concerning the entity (one-way communication)

Each person referenced in the RACI matrix is a *stakeholder* in the entity - which means that each link will also point to people who will need to be consulted, and at the least informed, about any changes to the entity. So in addition to identifying mutual cross-dependencies - a map of mutual responsibilities across the entire enterprise - this also provides us with the list of stakeholders that we need for architecture-governance or project-governance each time we reference the entity in an architecture cycle.

In principle this means literally every crosslink of mutual responsibility in the entire enterprise, changing continually at every level of the enterprise from abstract ideals to the moment-by-moment detail of real-time operations. So this is another one of these assessment-items that's impossibly huge: there's no way we could do it all, and it would be hopelessly out of date even if we did. Kind of pointless, really... and yet we *need* that information.

To get anywhere useful, we're going to need to partition a set of priorities – for which one key source will be the previous work on business-continuity (see p.130). Another approach is to embed the requisite information-gathering within any other architectural work going on at the time – any kind of assessment, right back to reviews of any of the work in the previous steps. If we make a habit of collecting the information as we go, in time it'll seem as if it collects itself.

But with a serious bit of sideways thinking, we ourselves wouldn't need to do the information-gathering: in classic programming terminology, we should include it 'by reference', not 'by value'. It's not really within our remit to do this work, and other people are already doing much of it anyway, in rosters, in team-assignments, and in the myriad of HR detail. It's actually the human analogue of the CMDB issues that we saw back in business-continuity planning: so if we can find a way to link in to the respective information-sources – ideally in real-time, as with the CMDB – then our responsibility-maps would update themselves.

Either way, we *do* need those 'response-ability'-maps, especially in the high-priority areas of the architecture: whichever way round we do it – whether by asking ourselves, asking others, or building some kind of automated self-update – the nominal questions we'll need are summarised in the lists below.

Responsibility as service

For each entity in scope:

- Who is *responsible* for the entity? - the 'responsible owner' who has personal accountability for the appropriate use and application of the entity in its service to the enterprise? If no-one is directly responsible for the entity, is there an implied responsibility, such as by role? If no-one appears to be responsible for the entity, what impact does this have on the effective use or application of the entity in the enterprise?
- In what ways do these 'responsible owner' accountabilities intersect with those for equivalent entities in other architecture-layers? - for example, operations responsibility versus those of a scheduler, line-manager, developer, business-unit manager, executive? In what ways do 'owner'-responsibilities for a single composite-entity intersect with 'owner'-responsibilities for collective sets of the underlying primitives or composites? - for example, responsibility for a specific business-process in which an IT-system is used versus responsibility for all of that type of IT-systems? Given that all of these represent distinct 'owner'-responsibilities for what is in effect the same real-world entity, how are the relations between these 'owners' managed and resolved?
- Who or what *assists* the 'responsible owner' in the use and application of the entity in the aims of the enterprise? In what form is this assistance provided? - for example, in person, by machines, within IT-systems? How and in what ways are these 'assists'-responsibilities shared across the enterprise?
- Who needs to be *consulted* on any changes to the entity, or to its use or application in the enterprise? For what reasons do they need to be consulted rather than merely informed? For which changes or uses, and at what timescales? What responsibilities does 'consulted' imply and entail in each case?
- Who needs to be *informed* on any changes to the entity, or to its use or application in the enterprise? For what reasons do

they need to be informed about such changes? For which changes or uses, and at what timescales? For what reasons should they only be informed rather than actively consulted? What responsibilities does this imply and entail in each case?

- Who needs to be consulted or informed *implicitly* about the entity – for example, in aggregate reports, or as a collective or composite with other entities? For what reasons do they need this relationship with the entity? For which changes or uses, and at what timescales? What responsibilities does this indirect relationship imply and entail in each case?
- Who should *not* be consulted or informed about changes to the entity? For what reasons? – for example, out of scope, or risk of 'information-overload'? What *absence* of responsibilities is implied in each case? In what ways does this absence of responsibilities serve the enterprise?
- In what ways, for what reasons, and at what timescales, are each of these responsibilities transferred from person to person? What mechanisms and processes exist to ensure that these transfers do take place? What mechanisms and processes exist to record, monitor and audit each responsibility and transfer of responsibility?
- Is each person *aware* of the respective responsibility? – for example, is it listed in the duties of a role, but without adequate description of what the responsibilities entail?
- What mechanisms and processes exist to ensure that the respective responsibilities are carried out effectively, in service to the enterprise? In what ways is the effectiveness of the responsibility monitored, measured and verified?
- In what ways does each of these personal responsibilities represent a service in person to the enterprise?

> Be slightly wary about how you ask some of these questions: most do have personal overtones, and in the wrong context could be taken as an insult or even a threat. If in doubt, present the more 'personal'-seeming questions as something for people to ask themselves, rather than as information you're aiming to collect from others.

Document the results as attributes for or links between the respective entities in the architecture repository, either by reference or by value. Record any related requirements, risks, opportunities or issues in the respective registers, and notify other stakeholders in those items accordingly.

Capability as service

For each entity in scope, assess the capabilities required to support the specified responsibility:

- What capabilities, competencies and skillsets are required either *as* the entity, *within* the entity, or to *use* or *apply* the entity within the enterprise? In what ways does the capability provide 'response-ability' to support or underlie the 'owner'-responsibilities and other responsibilities for the entity?
- If required capabilities, competencies or skillsets are not available to the enterprise in relation to the entity, what would need to be done to obtain or develop them?
- What mechanisms and processes exist to ensure that the respective responsibilities are assigned appropriately? – for example, that each person has the appropriate capability and 'response-ability' for the tasks? How and in what ways would changes in that 'response-ability' be monitored, and responsibilities re-assigned?
- In what ways are the capabilities and responsibilities 'of service' to the enterprise? In what ways does the perspective shift by viewing them *as* services to the enterprise? What are the consequences and implications of that shift in perspective?

Document the results as attributes for or links to the respective entities in the architecture repository, either by reference or by value. Once again, advise others as appropriate of any requirements, risks, opportunities and issues identified in this process.

Dealing with 'wicked problems'

The ***purpose*** of this section is to identify inherently-intractable 'wicked problems' in the enterprise, to identify the factors that render the problems intractable, and to assist in developing and implementing strategies and tactics to resolve them in practice.

Almost by definition, the range of ***people*** and skillsets that you'll need for this work cannot be predicted in advance. There will, however, be two distinct types: the subject-matter experts (SMEs) for each specialist area which you touch; and the social-network 'supernodes' who may not have personal detailed knowledge of some essential area, yet – to quote the old Yellow Pages advert – will always know "someone who does".

> By this stage most of the architecture team should themselves be 'supernodes' across a wide range of professional and expertise-

oriented social-networks within the enterprise. The architecture *is* the ongoing dialogue you share with others on architecture-related issues: all those contacts and personal connections that you've built up during the work so far will really pay off here.

The other absolute people-requirement for this work is overt support at very senior levels, preferably a CxO executive or the CEO. *You cannot do this work without it.*

By the very nature of the problems you address here, almost anything you do will cross organisational boundaries, tramp on much-defended turf, touch on 'taboo topics' and poke into some highly-politicised 'pain-points' – and if you don't have high-level authority and high-level protection, you're going to find yourself under full-on attack almost from the moment you start. So don't even *think* of trying to tackle this type of work without serious senior-level support behind you.

Cultivating a thick skin helps, too. As you'll no doubt discover the hard way, there's good reason why one well-known list of essential attributes for enterprise architects not only includes character-traits such as "diplomatic, strong people-skills", but "persistent, enduring" as well. Another important warning there!

The ***planning*** side of this work will depend on two key items: the trails of links and interdependencies in the architecture repository; and a solid understanding of 'soft-systems theory' - particularly the human aspects of complex systems.

Some of the sources we use for this in our own work include Peter Senge's *Fifth Discipline* materials; the VPEC-T (values, process, events, content, trust) methodology developed by Nigel Green and colleagues; the Cynefin model of organisational complexity, developed by Dave Snowden and others; the Spiral Dynamics model of transactions between worldviews or 'vMemes', based on value-systems analysis by sociologist Clare Graves in the 1950s; depth-foresight techniques such as Causal Layered Analysis, developed by Sohail Inayatullah and others; and our own research on power-issues as documented in the companion books *Power and Response-ability* and *SEMPER and SCORE*.

Reference-details for all of these are in the *Resources* section at the end of the chapter.

For this work, the ***practice*** will always be iterative: use the cycles-within-cycles governance for the architecture, and an Agile-type methodology for intervention design and implementation.

Once again, ***performance*** can only be measured in terms of the whole. Expectation-management will also be crucial here: most stakeholders will no doubt want a fixed, certain 'solution' to the problem, but by the very nature of 'wicked problems' - as we'll see below - no such static solution can exist. Resolution of a 'wicked problem' is not an achievable 'goal' as such, but is always an ongoing, ever-evolving *process* - and needs to be managed, monitored and measured as such.

Tame problems and wicked problems

The issues that we face in enterprise in enterprise architecture fall into two fundamentally different categories:

- *'tame' problems*: those to which identifiable analytic rules apply - including a so-called 'stopping rule' which determines completion and closure - and hence an explicit 'solution' which can be identified in advance
- *'wicked' problems*: those which are *inherently* dynamic, complex or chaotic, and for which no stable explicit 'solution' can exist

> One classic example of a wicked-problem is 'business/IT alignment', more accurately known as the 'business/IT divide'. One key reason as to *why* it becomes so 'wicked' is that the respective worldviews are radically different, and hence the respective definitions of 'success'.

In the terms of the Cynefin framework, tame-problems fall into the *simple* ('known') or *complicated* ('knowable') domains. They're rule-based, and can be resolved via a straightforward work-instruction, or a more sophisticated calculation or cross-reference. So they're well-suited to machine-based or IT-based solutions; and the way we get to that solution is via *analysis*.

But wicked-problems will fall into the Cynefin *complex* or *chaotic* domains, where reality is either emergent or a unique 'market of one'. Conventional analysis alone will not help us here: in fact it's probably *the* primary reason why an already difficult problem turns 'wicked'. What we need instead is a *synthesis* across of all the conflicting perspectives that in play in the context.

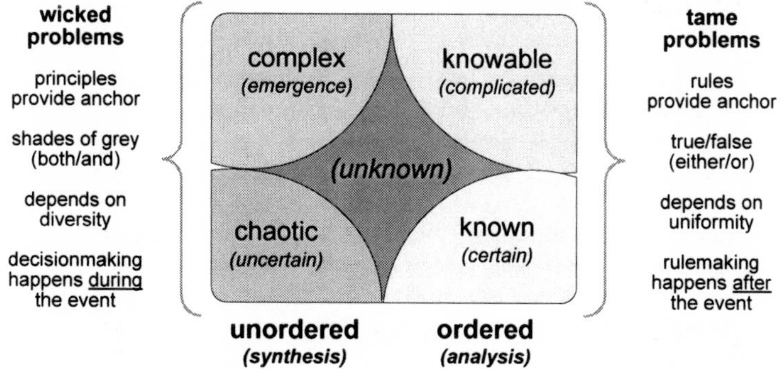

Cynefin framework: tame problems and wicked problems

Managers and others will so much want that every problem they face should be a 'tame' one, with a nice, easily-understandable, logical solution that can be provided once-and-for-all with some definable, predictable piece of IT or the like. But the painful reality is that real-world problems *are* 'wicked', rooted in ambiguity, in dynamic uncertainty, tensions of opposites, clashes of worldviews - and for those concerns, we need quite different skills and competencies than can at present be built into any viable IT system. So we perhaps need to give this point a bit more emphasis:

A wicked-problem cannot be solved by IT alone.

There *is* no permanent 'solution' to a wicked-problem: the very act of addressing the problem will, in itself, change the ways in which we experience the problem; and the underlying drivers are themselves changing all the time anyway. So anything we do will make it either better, or worse (or both, sometimes): the best we can aim for is to create some approach which is *self-evolving*, adapting itself to create a stream of transient, context-specific 'solutions', each aligned to the overall principles and purpose of the enterprise.

Every wicked-problem is also both a symptom and a cause of other wicked-problems. We can never 'fix' a wicked-problem in isolation: everything is connected to everything else, so we can *only* address it at the level of the whole.

Because the real world is inherently complex, it's probable that most real business problems *are* 'wicked', or have some significant component of 'wickedness' about them. There's also a crucial distinction between *technical complexity* - which sits more in the 'complicated', resolvable domain - and *social complexity* - which sits in the true 'complex' domain, and is *not* resolvable in any 'rational' manner. By the definition of 'enterprise', organisations are social structures: social-complexity is an inherent consequence of that - hence the inevitability of wicked-problems in business.

> There are a couple of very quick ways to *increase* the destructive 'wickedness' of a problem, that by now we'll have come across often in our architecture work: namely Taylorism, and IT-centrism.
>
> Taylorism's purported 'scientific management' causes problems because it tries to pretend that the complexity doesn't exist. The enterprise is a machine, it says; machines may be complicated, but they aren't complex; everything follows the rules. And since the rules have priority over everything else, anything which doesn't follow those rules is *wrong*, and should be punished accordingly. So because the real world *is* complex, there are lots of situations where the rules can't

work, and therefore don't work - hence lots of excuses for blame, for punishment, and for *seriously* wicked problems…

In essence, IT-centrism is a slightly more benign version of Taylorism: it doesn't view people as 'components of the machine' in quite the same way that Taylorism does, but it *does* assume that every problem has a rational, logical, definable solution, and hence that IT – as the epitome of rational action – is the answer to everything. Unfortunately, this doesn't actually work: as we saw earlier about skills, competencies, capabilities and decision-making (see p.53), almost all IT-systems are rule-based, and cannot handle true complexity. (True, some robotics and 'artificial intelligence' systems are beginning to get close to that level, but not within the price-brackets we're likely to see in business – not for a fair while yet, anyway.) The result is that either there's a futile attempt to identify every possible failure-condition – which can't succeed, because by definition there are an infinity of possible solutions to a wicked-problem – or else all the real complex-domain decisions are handballed on to the human operators, and then promptly ignored because it's not IT any more and hence 'out of scope'. If the operators don't have the skill and experience to *know* when this happens, and what to do about it when it does, we end up with lots of lame excuses about 'computer error' and the like – and, again, lots of buck-passing, lots of blame, and some seriously wicked problems.

The moral of this story? Many of the real-world issues we deal with in business are not rational: where they're not, don't rely only on 'rational' means alone to 'solve' them!

When we're dealing with any kind of social complexity, we're no longer in a predictable, 'rational' space; and the only *real* law is Murphy's anyway. So to tackle wicked-problems, we have to start from that fact: be aware of it, acknowledge it, and act accordingly.

Which is not easy, precisely *because* it's not rational when everyone expects – *demands* – that it 'should' be. So it's best to be ready for the painful fact that tackling any wicked-problem will almost invariably open up the proverbial 'can of worms': expect ruffled feathers, angry outbursts, screwed-up assumptions, nasty politicised surprises and lots and lots and *lots* of blame. We've seen full-on temper-tantrums at times – sometimes aimed at us personally, in classic 'shoot the messenger' style. Oh joys…

The great computing-industry consultant Gerry Weinberg summarised the architect's agony all too well in his classic *The Secrets of Consulting*: "It seemed that I had only two choices: to remain rational, and go crazy; or become irrational, and be called crazy. For years, I oscillated between those two poles of misery…". But, as he explains in the book: there *is* a way out of this dilemma: *become rational about the irrationality.* And *that's* what we aim to do here, in this section of the work.

Any 'pain-point' in the business will almost certainly be rooted in a wicked-problem of some kind; and the reason *why* it's causing pain is because someone's trying to 'control' the wicked-problem. Other than in fairly unusual and invariably short-lived conditions, the classic attempts at 'command and control' simply don't work with wicked-problems: at best, all they will do is paper over the cracks, making the problems harder to locate, harder to repair, and even more likely to cause a collapse into catastrophic failure:

There is no way to control a wicked-problem – but it *is* possible to guide it into a preferred direction.

Gerry Weinberg describes this as 'the Buffalo Bridle': a buffalo is *big*, heavy, far too strong to control; but you can make a buffalo go anywhere, as long as *it* wants to go there, and you can keep a buffalo out of anywhere, as long as *it* doesn't want to go there… the trick is in providing conditions such that the buffalo decides to do what we want it do. It's the same with a wicked-problem: we need to understand how it thinks – so to speak – and work *with* it to achieve the ends we need.

Wicked-problems, it seems, need wicked-solutions. It's not about control: it's a fair bit more subtle than that. Much if not most of conventional IT-architecture is about developing plans and checking for compliance against the architecture and suchlike; but again, that won't work here. Instead, we need to look much more closely at the *human* side of systems – because whilst that may be where the problems lie, it's also the only place from where we'll find any solutions. As Gerry Weinberg put it, whatever the problem looks like, and no matter how technical it may seem to be, it's *always* a 'people-problem'. Much of it is about motivation: people can go anywhere, do anything, solve any problem – *if* they want to do so. As architects, it's up to us to find the themes of structure and purpose that would help them want to do so.

We don't solve wicked-problems, as such: we provide conditions under which an appropriate solution can evolve *itself* from the context. For example:

- a wicked-problem is rooted in *dynamic uncertainty*: use the Cynefin framework to describe the differences between control and emergence, and the different skills and tactics needed in the complex-domain compared to those used in analysis in the 'knowable' (complicated) domain
- the uncertainty in a wicked-problem arises from the natural *tensions between polar opposites*, such as safety versus agility, or transparency versus security: use systems-theory to describe

that tension, and model the delays and feedback-loops and other transactions in the overall system

- other tensions in a wicked-problem arise from overt or covert *clashes of worldviews or value-systems*: use Spiral Dynamics or Causal Layered Analysis to identify and describe the respective value-systems, and specify 'translations' between the respective worldviews and the appropriate leadership tactics to use with each
- a common barrier against resolving a wicked-problem is *lack of trust* between stakeholders and stakeholder-groups: use the SEMPER diagnostic to measure and monitor the scale and domain of the difficulty; use VPEC-T and other sense-making techniques to identify the source, and to begin to ease the embedded tension

A more easily-resolvable source of wicked-problem tensions arises from confusions and disagreements over terminology. As the custodians of the common glossary and thesaurus, the architecture unit can have a key role to play here: in particular, the thesaurus makes it possible to accept multiple definitions as equally 'true', once we document the context-specific meanings and the links or conflicts between them.

One key to resolving wicked-problems is to recognise that there is no '*the* solution' - only an infinite variety of '*a* solution' which may each be 'better' or 'worse', good enough or not good enough, dependent on the exact balance of tensions at the time. That balance is always changing, over time, such that a 'best' solution at one time might be a 'worst' at another - hence the 'wickedness' of the problem. So we might design as if for a conventional 'tame' architectural problem, but we do so with the clear knowledge that it will need review and rebuild on a regular basis; and wherever practicable we would build with a 'safe-fail' approach (see p.134), to allow the solution to fall back 'gracefully' when it does fail - which, in the case of a wicked-problem, it always will.

But the real key to making wicked-problems manageable resides in *trust*. Anything we can do to help build trust will make wicked-problems easier - if only in terms of easier to bear, easier to accept, easier to live with. For architects, with our uncomfortable 'pig-in-the-middle' position in so many inter-silo arguments, this is why diplomacy and dialogue are so important: if we do it right, we literally create and carry that trust with us from place to place within the enterprise.

To identify what to do with a wicked-problem, and to make it easier to review in future, we need first to identify and document the drivers that underlie it. Then, using the 'pain-point' symptom to specify the start-point on the framework, we spiral-out from there in successive architecture-iterations, further characterising the issues, and thence allow an appropriate instance of 'solution' to emerge from the work itself.

Identifying 'wickedness'

A context is inherently 'wicked' if any of the following conditions apply:

- Are there any direct conflicts between any of the major drivers in the context? In particular, are any of the drivers - especially core-values - in *inherent* direct opposition to each other?
- Are there any fundamental differences in perspectives and worldviews between key groups of stakeholders? - for example, management versus operations, business versus IT, etc? Are there any fundamental 'win/lose' framings of relationships, that would characteristically enforce a conflict between stakeholder groups?
- Is it difficult or apparently impossible to define or derive a single 'correct' view of the context, that can be agreed upon by all parties? Are there multiple, conflicting views of the causes of the problem? Is it difficult or impossible to define and agree upon a single set of criteria for 'success' in the context?
- Is there evidence of inappropriate models or mindsets being brought to bear upon the context? - for example, the 'Taylorist trap' of issues escalated away from the hands-on knowledge needed to resolve a practical problem?
- Is there a significant degree of ambiguity or uncertainty about the context? Are key data or information-items either missing or inherently uncertain? Is there a strong political or other pressure to deliver a once-and-for-all 'solution' for the context, even though there is a high degree of ambiguity?
- Is the context highly politicised, especially with significant amounts of finger-pointing and 'other-blame'? Are there any strong ideological, cultural or economic constraints on the context? Is there a high or significant resistance to change amongst one or more key groups of stakeholders?
- Do the problems in the context appear to be symptoms of other complex yet interrelated problems?

- Is the context a 'pain-point' which never seems to be resolved, no matter how many attempts have been made to fix it?

Document the values and their conflicts in the respective parts of the architecture-repository - usually either the row-0 layer or the 'decisions' column. Record any identifiable 'wickedness' in the risks-register, and also note the context in the issues-register as an item requiring regular review.

Resolving wicked problems

To identify a workable 'solution' for a wicked-problem, first identify and document the drivers as above. Use the 'pain-point' symptom to specify the start-point on the framework, and then spiral-out from there in successive architecture-iterations. Once the 'solution' emerges, derive requirements and implementation-designs in the usual way

> Once again, the architect role here is usually that of decision-support – *not* decision-making. By the nature of wicked-problems, any solutions will often be highly politicised, and may need the full authority of the executive to cut through the arguments to reach a workable agreement. If you *are* asked to act as arbiter, make sure that all parties involved agree to this, otherwise you'll almost certainly be accused of taking sides – not recommended!

Note that almost all 'solutions' to wicked-problems will require some form of manual intervention and medium- to high- skill-levels and competencies in some parts of the process - do *not* expect to be able to build an IT-only solution for any wicked-problem. Clear guidelines will also be needed to enable those people to interpret boundary-conditions and to enable 'safe-fail' fallback as the tensions between the drivers shift within day-to-day practice.

Enhancing enterprise effectiveness

The ***purpose*** of this section is to explore options to enhance the overall effectiveness of any aspect of the enterprise, by optimising the trade-offs between the various dimensions of effectiveness.

> As we saw back right back at the start, in the initial exploration of the strategic role of architecture (see p.8), the core business-purpose of all enterprise architecture is to improve overall effectiveness – not just efficiency on its own, for example, but all strands, optimised, in balance, working together across the whole.
>
> These key concepts on effectiveness at the whole-of-enterprise level are explored in more depth in *SEMPER and SCORE* – whose main

> emphasis is on enterprise effectiveness – and also in *Real Enterprise Architecture*: see those books for more details on this.

As before, the ***people*** you'll need here may include anyone, with any appropriate skillset - in this context because the trade-offs between the effectiveness dimensions may touch any point or any activity in the enterprise.

The ***planning*** will again draw on the crosslinks in the architecture repository, following the trails of connections to identify options and opportunities that could enhance any aspect of effectiveness within the selected scope.

> This is yet another area where assessments could stretch to infinity! For sanity's sake, always define a cut-off point for the assessment-phases of an iteration, either by placing explicit boundaries on scope, or a specific limit on time or budget before you switch over to doing the gap-analysis and requirements for change.

The ***practice*** should again follow the standard architecture cycle. In general, every iteration will require its own business-purpose and business-value, though in many cases you'll be able to merge this work into other architecture activities as appropriate.

By this stage of architecture-development there should be few if any *major* change-projects - because most of those needs should already have been addressed earlier - but these assessments may well spawn a fair range of small amendments and restructures, especially at the operations level. As usual, these too should be managed in accordance with the standard change-governance procedures linked to the architecture-cycle.

The key criteria for ***performance*** here are demonstrable improvements in measures for effectiveness in the specified context.

Enhancing effectiveness

The core of the work in this section revolves around those five keywords for effectiveness: efficient, reliable, elegant, appropriate, integrated. We use them as a review-frame across any and every aspect of the enterprise: we apply them to *everything*; use them as tests and touchpoints for everything, as metrics for everything; we note how these threads or dimensions interweave with each other; we keep coming back to them, again and again.

We also use those keywords to trigger ideas about what we might call 'derived outcomes' of effectiveness: themes such as improved agility, adaptability to change, responsiveness to customers or to suppliers, or shorter product-development cycles. These are likely to vary from one organisation to another: for example, a not-for-profit organisation dealing with world-wide disaster management may well need high agility, but might not develop any products of its own. The enterprise values and brief discussions with key stakeholders should indicate which derived-outcomes are most likely to be relevant in the organisation and enterprise.

Overall, it's a very simple checklist, but a surprisingly powerful one: use it wherever you can in your architecture work.

> There's only one additional proviso here: always remember to anchor that quest for effectiveness back to its anchors in the enterprise vision, values, principles and key guiding constraints. Doing this should be straightforward enough, given the sheer volume of links and connections that you'll have gathered by now in the architecture repository: in a good architecture toolset, you should be able to build the requisite models automatically. But do take care in this, because it's so easy to fall back into thinking only in terms of the immediate scope: the latter would give us *local* effectiveness – optimised for the immediate context – but probably not optimised for effectiveness across the whole, which is our real architectural need. The inverse of an old slogan from the environmental movement may help us maintain our 'ecosystem' here: "act local, think global"!

Reviewing effectiveness, enhancing agility

For any given context:

- What options exist to enhance and optimise *efficiency* in this context? Are there any means to make better use of the available resources?
- What options exist to enhance and optimise *reliability* in this context? Are there any means to provide more certainty that the context can be relied upon to deliver the required results?
- What options exist to enhance *elegance* in this context - the human factors? Are there any options to augment 'elegance' in the scientific sense - to simplify, to clarify, to enhance consistency and re-use? What means exist to develop personal skills and knowledge, to enhance understanding and awareness? What options exist for systems and processes to adapt to and make best use of individual difference and individual skills? - for example, ergonomics and accessibility design, self-adapting performance-support systems and decision-support systems?
- What options exist to enhance and optimise *appropriateness* in this context? Are there any additional means to link this context more strongly to the enterprise vision, values and

principles, such that it more powerfully supports and sustains the overall purpose of the enterprise? By what means would it be practicable to enhance awareness of, capability for, and monitoring of alignment to each key enterprise-value in this context?

- What options exist to enhance and optimise *integration* in this context? Are there any additional means to ensure that everything in this context is linked to and supports the integration of the whole *as* whole?
- Given the above, in what ways could any of these options be used to enhance 'derived outcomes' such as agility, responsiveness and reduced time-to-market, both within this context, and in areas impacted by this context?

Use these questions to derive content for 'what if' scenarios, which should be modelled and documented in the architecture toolset in the usual way, and used as the basis for further discussion and assessment. As per the architecture cycle, use gap-analysis to derive change-requirements, and work with the respective stakeholders to expand these requirements into high-level designs, change-projects and so on. Document any risks, opportunities and issues in the respective registers, and ensure that these items are included in any subsequent reviews.

Resources

📖 'Fifth Discipline' series on systems-thinking in business practice: see Peter M Sengé et al, *The Fifth Discipline: the art and practice of the learning organization* (Nicholas Brealey Publishing, 1990); *The Fifth Discipline Fieldbook: strategies and tools for building a learning organization* (Nicholas Brealey Publishing, 1994); and *The Dance of Change: the challenges of sustaining momentum in learning organizations* (Nicholas Brealey Publishing, 1999)

🕸 'Fifth Discipline' systems-thinking resources: see www.fieldbook.com

📖 Systems-principles: see Tom Graves, *The Service-Oriented Enterprise: enterprise architecture and viable services* (Tetradian, 2009)

📖 Stafford Beer 'Viable Systems Model' as an organisational structure: see Patrick Hoverstadt, *The Fractal Organization: creating sustainable organizations with the Viable System Model* (Wiley, 2008)

- Human factors in enterprise architecture: see Tom Graves, *Power and Response-ability: the human side of systems* (Tetradian, 2008)
- Effectiveness as a driver for enterprise architecture: see Tom Graves, *SEMPER and SCORE: enhancing enterprise effectiveness* (Tetradian, 2008)
- 'Wicked problems': see Wikipedia summary at en.wikipedia.org/wiki/Wicked_problem and more detail at Cognexus: www.cognexus.org – particularly the article 'Wicked Problems and Social Complexity' at cognexus.org/wpf/wickedproblems.pdf
- VPEC-T methodology: see Nigel Green and Carl Bate, *Lost in Translation: a handbook for information systems in the 21st century* (Evolved Technologist Press, 2008)
- VPEC-T resources: see www.LIThandbook.com
- Cynefin framework: see Wikipedia summary at en.wikipedia.org/wiki/Cynefin and more detail at Cognitive Edge: www.cognitive-edge.com
- Spiral Dynamics: see Don Beck and Chris Cowan, *Spiral Dynamics: mastering values, leadership and change* (Blackwell, 1996)
- Spiral Dynamics resources: see www.spiraldynamics.com (National Values Center), www.spiraldynamics.net (Spiral Dynamics Integral) and Wikipedia summary at en.wikipedia.org/wiki/Spiral_Dynamics
- Causal Layered Analysis: see Sohail Inayatullah, www.metafuture.org/Articles/CausalLayeredAnalysis.htm
- Working with the non-rational in consulting: see Gerald M Weinberg, *The Secrets of Consulting: a guide to giving and getting advice successfully* (Dorset House, 1986)
- Whole-of-enterprise architecture: see Tom Graves, *Real Enterprise Architecture: beyond IT to the whole enterprise* (Tetradian, 2008)

WHAT NEXT?

Once we've completed that last step, we've gone as far as the standard maturity-model will take us. So what happens next?

The first point, perhaps, is to recognise that the architecture doesn't stop there, just because we've reached some magic milestone. It isn't a project: it's a continual quest for new ways to enhance enterprise effectiveness in the face of continual change.

What we *have* done in all this work - in addition to guiding consistency and change throughout the enterprise - is that we've gathered together a powerful and versatile set of tools:

- to describe enterprise vision, values and culture - see p.33
- to describe its key compliance and other constraints - see p.41
- to model the core assets, locations, events, functions, capabilities, services and decisions - see p.43 and p.48
- to create systems for engagement and architecture governance - see p.57 and p.60
- to partition activities into consistent 'business systems' and their supporting 'information systems' - see p.68 and p.71
- to optimise across any aspect of a business-system - see p.73
- to guide compliance in the overall process of change - see p.85
- to extend architecture across the whole enterprise - see p.95
- to explore how strategy interacts with change and innovation - see p.100 and p.107
- to use service-concepts 'top-down' to guide implementation trade-offs and quality-compliance - see p.110 and p.117
- to use service-concepts 'bottom-up' for real-time problem-escalation and load-balancing - see p.125 and p.128
- to guide business-continuity planning and 'safe-fail' design - see p.131 and p.134
- to review and sustain enterprise values from the operations perspective - see p.138
- to extend service-concepts to the whole enterprise and to the human side of systems - see p.144 and p.147
- to deal with 'pain-points' and 'wicked problems' - see p.151
- to review and extend effectiveness in any context - see p.159

You'll no doubt need to revisit all of those themes from time to time, depending on what's going on in the enterprise and where the flow of change seems to be heading at each moment. It's also important to be pro-active, too, and seek out new opportunities to enhance innovation and effectiveness wherever they may be found.

Either way, use that list above as a 'menu' of options from which you can choose at each point, to keep developing the architecture and embedding it within the enterprise.

So the focus here is on enhancing enterprise agility and overall effectiveness, leveraging from all the architecture work that has gone on before. There is enormous business-value to be gained from this work: and assuming that you *have* been documenting it as you've gone along, you can prove that value, too.

Yet there is still more that we can do, to lift that value to even greater heights. But we should *only* do it if and when the enterprise itself is ready to take it on – because, as we saw with some of the other architecture-maturity issues, if we try to do the work too early, we risk causing more harm than good.

The key criterion for this extension to architecture is that *the enterprise must be able, ready and willing to give up command and control* in the respective areas of its business. If not, fine: it's not a value judgement, because in some industries, and certainly in some areas of business, the law itself may demand some form of rigid control, whether or not the enterprise would choose otherwise. It's just that a slackening-off in these two emphases will open up new options for the enterprise and its architecture.

Once again, there's more explanation of these themes and their business implications in the companion books *SEMPER and SCORE* and *Power and Response-ability*.

Releasing control, to make allowance for – and use of – individual skills and difference, is one of the key criteria in attaining a level-4 on the SEMPER scale, and enables reliable operation in the Cynefin complex-domain; and relinquishing command, so as to support principle-based decision-making by individuals, is a key criterion for attaining SEMPER level-5 in any given area, and is central to viable operation in the Cynefin chaotic-domain. Neither of these are mandatory in any enterprise, and would be very unlikely to need to apply to all aspects of its operations; yet they're also the key factors in changing a middle-ranking 'best practice' business to one that ranks well above the rest, and in turn will enable the good to become truly great.

As architects, those cultural changes themselves are not within our own remit, but we *can* identify the areas where small changes of this kind can make the most difference – for everyone's benefit.

In architecture terms, most of what we do in the early stages of maturity is 'command and control': we define a reference architecture, and strive to ensure that change-projects comply with it. As maturity develops, we tackle more and more contexts in which either command or control are the core sources of difficulty - as is often the case in wicked-problems, for example - or where a loosening of mandated compliance is central to solving a problem - as it is in many quality-management contexts.

At this stage, though, we also need to apply that same thinking to the architecture itself. Relinquishing an overly possessive 'ownership' control over the architecture, for example, will permit a shift towards a 'hands-off' approach to architecture development, that can greatly reduce the day-to-day architecture workload, freeing architects to concentrate on the 'big-picture' direction of the overall enterprise; and that approach in turn depends on relinquishing command, instead developing the overall architecture through a more intensive and more inclusive emphasis on *dialogue*, with all stakeholders in the architecture as co-equal peers.

So these last two sections of the book will explore those two themes: operating a 'hands-off' architecture; and engaging the enterprise in extending and enhancing the *relevance* of architecture within its everyday working life.

Hands-off architecture

When the going gets tough, the tough have the sense to let go of trying to control it all, and turn to a more subtle form of management instead. This is certainly true of enterprise-scale architecture: there suddenly comes a point where it's all become too big, too much happening, too fast; the architecture team itself has become too big, too complex; enforcing compliance just takes too much time, too much effort; and there's an inexorable sense of sliding further and further backwards... That's when we need to shift to a 'hands-off' approach, allowing some aspects of the architecture to emerge in a natural way from the complexity itself.

> *Important*: Use of a 'hands-off' strategy will succeed only if the architecture and programme-management capabilities and processes, and the enterprise itself, are all mature enough to support it. In the appropriate contexts, it does work extremely well; but in an inappropriate context, or with an immature architecture, it could well result in catastrophic chaos. We've seen a fair few examples where people have tried to do it too early – in one instance solely as a cost-cutting exercise, which was a bad mistake from the start – and the

results were always messy, painful and expensive. *Not* recommended... Test the waters with a small, local experiment, perhaps, but don't try it on a full enterprise-wide scale unless you *know* you're ready.

So please *do* heed this warning: do *not* attempt to do hands-off architecture unless the opportunities, risks and trade-offs are fully understood by all concerned, and addressed appropriately in practice.

On the surface, the main reason for using a 'hands-off' architecture is to support agility and innovation. But more subtly, it's also about reinforcement of responsibility in the overall enterprise. It isn't 'our' architecture anyway: we're just its custodians – it belongs to the enterprise, not to us – and now that we've brought the architecture up to this level of maturity, it's time to hand that responsibility back to its true owners.

When done properly, this makes life easier for everyone. The architecture-compliance workload – the dreaded role of 'architecture police' – shrinks right down to the point where it can be handled by a much smaller team; the domain-architects are freed to go back to their preferred areas of expertise, leaving only a small core to concentrate on architecture at the enterprise-wide scope. Unlike the earlier stages, there's no predefined plan or 'blueprint' for the architecture. Instead, the effective architecture is allowed to emerge organically in relation to a set of specific and clearly-enunciated architectural principles, emphasising overall *effectiveness* for each project in relation to the whole.

In essence it's an extension of the existing work on guiding change with the Programme Management Office – see p.85. Most of the responsibility for architecture assessment – equivalent to Phases A to D in the main architecture-cycle – is passed to project sponsors, domain-architects and designers. The architecture unit maintains a watching brief over projects that pass through the Programme Management Office – the equivalent of Phase G in the main cycle – and will intervene with advice, suggestions and requests for change only where appropriate, in line with the overall aims for the architecture. The architecture unit also uses the in-progress and completed projects as a source of information for reviews of the architecture itself – equivalent to Phase H in the main cycle.

The overall process resembles that for a building project in a city-planning context

- the 'developer' is the project-sponsor and project-team
- the 'planning authority' is the Programme Management Office
- the architecture unit maintains the equivalent of the 'city plan'

Just as for a building-project in city-planning, each managed enterprise-project has to pass through a number of go/no-go 'gateways'. At each gateway:

- the developer presents to the planning-authority a description of how the project will satisfy any mandatory requirements ('building regulations') and the architectural principles ('planning approval')
- if the proposal does not satisfy any of the mandatory requirements, it is rejected and returned to the developer for reassessment
- if the proposal passes mandatory requirements, the planning-authority publish the description, to allow other sponsors and stakeholders to comment, and optionally collaborate on amending their own projects
- the planning-authority also notifies the architecture unit, as a key stakeholder in all projects, to review the proposal and intervene as appropriate - see 'Project-gateway notification and response', p.171
- if any disputes or concerns arise from the stakeholders, the PMO acts as a tribunal, with the architecture team in the role of expert advisor, to arrive at a negotiated agreement on changes to the project.

This process repeats at each project-gateway, dependent on the programme-management methodology and the governance-rules in use.

Assuming that the project then passes successfully through each gateway to completion, the sponsor presents a final 'as-built' description that summarises what was actually done over the intervening period. This allows the architecture team to again review the impact and 'lessons learned' for the overall architecture of the enterprise - see 'Project-completion', p.172 - which then feeds back into the architecture models, principles and guidelines to be used by subsequent projects.

Preparation for hands-off architecture

Successful hands-off architecture depends on a number of key items and attributes:

- a clear set of *principles, guidelines* and *governance-rules* exist and are publicly available to all potential developers: these should be developed and authorised as for the main architecture - see p.37 and p.60

- an explicit set of *reference-frameworks* for the context exist and are publicly available, together with guidance for their use - see p.18
- shared facilities to capture, store, review and link between *requirements, issues, risks, dispensations* and the like exist and are generally available - see p.19
- facilities and mechanisms to support *engagement* by and with developers in the architecture are available and generally used - see p.57

As with the main architecture preliminaries - see p.4 onwards - you should expect to re-assess and, where necessary, update the principles, reference-frameworks and governance-rules at regular intervals - certainly at least once each year - and publish any changes through the same mechanisms.

Preparation review

- What engagement do projects already have in your existing architecture? What else would they need in order to take on their responsibilities in a hands-off architecture?
- What reference-frameworks do you have available that would be suitable for general use in a hands-off architecture? What scope do they each cover? What governances procedures and processes would they require for general use?
- How much of your existing architecture - particularly principles, guidelines and reference-frameworks - is published and generally accessible throughout the enterprise? What other information would be need to be published, and in what forms, to support a hands-off architecture?
- To what extent are projects and Programme Management Office ready and able to do their own architectural assessments? What could you do to extend that capability? What scope would a hands-off architecture apply, in which projects and which segments of programme-management?
- By what processes and facilities would you garner updates for the architecture itself? What governance would be required for this? By what means would you publicise and promulgate updates for a hands-off architecture?
- From the above, to what extent are you ready to run a hands-off architecture? What would you need to do - what would need to change - to make it more viable? What level of maturity would be needed in the existing architecture to make

this happen? What amendments to architecture-governance and project-governance would be required?

- How would you describe and present to management the business-case for a hands-off architecture? To what scope within the enterprise would this business-case apply?

Present the business-case, and - when approved - implement the required facilities and governance-changes to publicise the architecture changes and hand over to Programme Management.

Project-gateway notification and response

The 'hands-off' process is one of management by exception, rather than by routine intervention and control as in the main 'hands-on' methodology.

The initial trigger for the process is the arrival of a Project Architectural Description document. This is provided by the project sponsor or project-manager via the Programme Management Office, and should describe how the project will conform to the published mandatory rules, principles and reference-frameworks, and also describe any applications or innovations that might be relevant to the overall architecture for the enterprise.

> The architecture team may well have provided some assistance to the project before this happens, but the whole aim here is that the onus for getting it right should be on the project team rather than the architecture unit – hence 'hands-off' architecture.

On receipt of the document, you would then carry out a brief review of the description, to assess any possible issues, and then return the results of the review to the project sponsor via the Programme Management Office. Sometimes the issue will be that a project's intentions clash with the architecture or with another project, but it might also be that they're introducing an innovation that could be valuable elsewhere, and that you're asking their advice on how best to do this - in other words, it should always be portrayed as a two-way street, not an 'edict from above'.

Project-gateway review

On receipt of the project Architecture Description Statement, use the following checklist to review the content:

- In what ways, and to what extent, does the project comply with the published architecture standards? Where the standards are not mandatory, are the deviations from the recommended or advised standards acceptable? What implications would those variances have for the architecture as a whole?

- If there are significant variances from standards, would an architecture-dispensation be required? – for example, if the mandated or recommended standard is not technically feasible or available in that specific context, or is over-ruled by local laws and ordinances? If so, how should the dispensation be described and documented, and what conditions and review-periods should be applied to that dispensation?
- Are there are direct clashes or conflicts with any other projects? – for example, each needing exclusive usage or control of the same physical equipment or the same virtual space? If so, what would need to be done by each project to resolve the clash?
- Is there any potential for synergies with other projects? – for example, using the same type of equipment, software applications or development-tools, or touching the same business-systems or business areas? If so, what changes would be needed in each project to optimise those synergies?
- Is the project introducing innovations of any kind – asset, function, location-category, capability, event-type, business-rule or composite – which could be applied or re-used within the overall architecture? If so, what further information would the architecture unit need from the project in order to do so?

If any issues are identified, document the results in an Architecture Position Statement and, if appropriate, an Architecture Dispensation Statement, and return these to the PMO, together with a request for negotiation with the project if so required.

The outcome of this review may include recommended changes to the project or to a group of projects; a formal dispensation; or changes to the architecture itself – which may in turn trigger new architecture cycles, and also updates to the published architecture principles and guidelines. Update the architecture registers for risks, opportunities, issues and dispensations as appropriate.

Project-completion

Each project should also create a similar architecture description at the end of the project implementation, as part of their own 'lessons learned' review. The aim here is to notify the architecture unit about what was actually implemented and delivered – which may not be the same as in the original plan.

There's no response-document required here, of course, because the project is over and done with – you can't change that. But what you *can* do is update the architecture, and again let other projects know about any lessons learned from the exercise. It's all part of maintaining stakeholder engagement in the development of the architecture, as an *enterprise-wide* shared resource.

The review here is essentially the same as at the end of any other project for which the architecture unit has provided guidance - see p.90. In principle the receipt of the Description document should trigger its own architecture lessons-learned review, but in practice the document would more usually be included as part of the content for the next regular review, much as for other types of simultaneous architecture-cycles - see p.83.

As at the end of the project-gateway review, this may trigger new architecture cycles, or updates to the published architecture principles, guidelines and reference-frameworks.

Architecture as relevance

Having relinquished control in hands-off architecture, the final step is to relinquish command as well.

As architects we may have a better overview of the enterprise than most people, but that doesn't make us any more 'special' than anyone else. The only area we know well is architecture, "a body of knowledge about enterprise structure and purpose": we don't know much of the fine detail about how the enterprise *really* works - the people who *do* know that are the specialists and those who work at the 'coal-face' out in the operations-space. So whilst we may sit up at the top of the tower, sharing the time of day with strategists and senior executives, all it really means is that we, like they, have our own job to do in support of the enterprise. We have neither right nor reason to 'command' others about *anything* - even architecture. And a bit of humility and respect on our part can go a long way in helping the overall cause of the enterprise…

So it's useful here to go right back to where we started, to take note of two essentials for the *real* architecture of the enterprise:

- You'll need to engage with stakeholders - see p.11
- It's really about dialogue - see p.12

This architecture isn't something we've created on our own: we've *co-created* it with everyone else with whom we've worked. All those domain-architects and designers and project-managers and risk-managers and knowledge-managers and personnel specialists and operations specialists and all the others listed in all those 'People' sections in the steps above in this book – and no doubt many, many others as well. It isn't 'our' architecture: it belongs to everyone in the enterprise.

So let go; let go of command. Instead, commit to *engagement,* commit to *dialogue,* and allow the architecture to evolve and emerge from the enterprise itself.

You'll have tackled the basics of this already, in the earlier work on engagement – see p.57. You'll also have built on that base in the meantime, such as with the publishing-facilities built into your architecture-toolset and the like. So the following sections suggest some themes you might find useful to take this further, and keep the architecture relevant in people's working lives.

Conferences

What are the core architectural issues people are facing across the enterprise? Much of the time, we don't actually know: we can assess market trends, we can review best-practice inside the organisation and elsewhere, we can analyse, often in great depth; but even then the results may well be little more than a guess…

To find out what's really needed, we have to *ask*. And more than just ask: as suggested in that quote from Dave Snowden earlier, people often only know what they know when they need to know it; often they know what they want only when they see it, and also often don't even know *that* they want it till they see it.

So a useful tactic here is to organise a regular architecture conference, partly to promote and explain the architecture and its role, but also to engage others at all levels in *their* views on the architecture and where it should be going so as to best serve the needs of the enterprise. Such conferences work particularly well if they are centred around one or more of the enterprise 'pervasives':

- security and safety, in any or all of its forms
- quality – again, in any or all of its forms
- business-continuity and risk-management
- privacy and trust
- customer orientation or service orientation
- agility and responsiveness
- end-to-end process-integration
- innovation and experimentation

• the practical meaning and implication of 'value'

In the early stages, it's usually best to set up a formal agenda; but as architecture-maturity increases across the enterprise, and there is more experience with managing the architecture in a more open and inclusive style, it's useful also to start relinquishing control of the agenda, until the broader enterprise claims full ownership of that as well.

There are a variety of formal models for these more open-format conferences, as summarised in Martin Leith's well-known 'Guide to Large Group Interventions'. Of these, perhaps the most extreme is Harrison Owen's 'Open Space Technology': it draws from the insight that for many people, the most valuable part of a conference is the gap between formal sessions - so Open Space is a type of conference that consists entirely of 'gap'. There is no formal agenda: instead, attendees take responsibility to present topics that have direct meaning for them. People then 'vote with their feet', moving between sessions until they gravitate to a group which has relevance for their own work-interests. The end-result - if it's done right - is a huge outpouring of energy, with active, personal commitment to tackling the self-chosen tasks.

> The "if it's done right" is critical here, because the process depends entirely on openness, on the organisers and the relevant management fully letting go of the agenda, and instead allowing it to emerge naturally from the context and from the attendees themselves.
>
> Open Space can be downright scary in that regard – we never know in advance what the outcome will be. But that almost anarchic freedom and uncertainty is also the key to its real power: any attempt to control it will not only block any possibility of emergence, but will likely also lead to a feeling of betrayal, and an entrenched cynicism and loss of trust that could echo on for months or years. Open Space is probably the most powerful of all the 'large group interventions', yet it should *only* be used where there's full support and commitment to the process; if there's any significant risk that the promise of support will be withdrawn – especially in the middle of the process itself – it would be safer to use one of the more 'controlled' techniques such as Delphi or Future Search instead.

Communities of practice

The right kind of conference will also help create the right kind of communities-of-practice that the enterprise needs. Each group of specialists will typically need to form its own explicit community, to share best-practices and worst-practices, to look for advice on how to solve specific problems, to develop each others' skills and the skills of newcomers, and to develop the praxis as a whole. To the enterprise, each community-of-practice is a key part of its own knowledge-management: it *needs* those communities-of-practice.

> The doyen of studies on communities-of-practice is independent researcher Etienne Wenger: "the basic idea is that human knowing is fundamentally a social act". His website at www.ewenger.com/theory provides more of the theoretical background, whilst his books such as *Cultivating Communities of Practice* (co-authored with Richard McDermott and William Snyder) explain more about how to put the theory into practice. Recommended.

There are, however, a few practical concerns from the organisation's perspective. These include:

- Communities of practice succeed *because* they are enterprises in their own right. They intersect with the organisation, and support the organisation, but do not 'belong' to it. The organisation can foster them, and support them in turn, but will destroy their value if it tries to control or possess them.
- In most cases, the knowledge underpinning each specialism and skill will extend across almost every kind of border: business-unit, organisation, nation, language, culture, whatever. This also means that those conversations must be able to cross those borders – which may represent a security-risk in several different senses. Yet closing the borders also limits the knowledge that the organisation may gain from the community-of-practice. The trade-offs here are not simple, and need careful management by all parties involved.
- For those reasons above, many communities-of-practice will operate either informally or as a 'shadow network': bringing them out into the light can actually destroy them. Similarly, the organisation can rarely create a new community-of-practice to order – the community devolves from *personal* responsibility and commitment, not formal authority.

The architecture can help in this, by identifying capabilities that use or could use such communities; identifying likely candidates from responsibility-assignments to related architecture-entities; and using social-network maps to identify probable 'supernodes' for the communities' social-networks. We can also use the architecture itself to help communities to become more aware of the security risks, and also of other opportunities that could help the community and the enterprise alike. In turn, through dialogue, the communities can feed key information back into the architecture of the enterprise: *everyone* wins.

Communication

Communities-of-practice are extremely valuable, yet themselves are only one form of communication and organisational learning – the *other* half of the enterprise's 'information technology'. Which brings us back to a central theme for enterprise architecture:

The dialogue about architecture *is* the architecture.

The models are useful: but it's about more than just models. Governance-rules are important: but it's not just about governance. Change is a key driver: but it's not solely about managing change. *The architecture is the dialogue; the dialogue is the architecture.*

Hence we need more than just a 'Communication Plan' for architecture: the multi-way, multi-faceted communication we need is both the source and the destination for the architecture. Communication is everywhere; communication is everything.

In effect, enterprise-architecture itself is another of the enterprise 'pervasives' – or more accurately, the *idea* of whole-of-enterprise integration that the architecture presents and promotes is the real 'pervasive' here. So the same practical concerns apply to architecture as for all other 'pervasive' themes:

- we need explicit means to *develop awareness of architecture* as a pervasive principle
- we need to *develop architecture capability* across the enterprise
- we need to ensure that the *architecture capability is used* throughout the enterprise
- we need to *verify and audit* that the architecture principles have been applied appropriately in practice

The last two of these have been our main focus so far: that was the reasoning behind the architecture cycle and its integration into the programme- and project-management cycles. We now *know* how to do those in a controlled environment. But as we relinquish a rigid control of the architecture, moving towards a more open, hands-off approach, we also need much more emphasis on the first pair of concerns: develop architecture awareness, and develop architecture capability. Hence the *need* for dialogue.

Conferences and training-sessions and the like will support the development of capability: that part is relatively straightforward, and we already know how to do that, *if* the awareness and the recognition of the need is already there. But how do we develop that awareness in the first place?

Some of this you'll have had to do already, just to get started with the architecture practice: building the business-case, getting the executives to understand the underlying ideas, and so on. Then there's been all the work around maintaining and publishing the glossary, thesaurus, reference-models, blueprints, roadmaps, and all the architecture-governance rules to go with them. But for most of the current crop of architecture-toolsets, that's still only 'one-way', broadcast-style publishing: no interaction, no *dialogue*. And we need that dialogue to happen, and happen *as* a true dialogue.

One way to take this further is to look at how other 'pervasives' tackle the same problems - particularly knowledge-management and change-management, who deal with much the same kinds of concerns as our own.

> Unlike the enterprise architecture domain, which is still overly dominated by obsessions about computer-based IT, other 'pervasive'-domains such as change-management and the like already provide many tools and techniques to promote and enhance the *human* 'information technology' of knowledge-acquisition and knowledge-sharing.
>
> For example, Senge's *The Dance of Change* and Collison and Parcell's *Learning to Fly* – our source for those notes earlier on the US Army's 'After Action Review' process – are both packed with proven examples of how to create engagement and dialogue in practice, across a wide variety of often 'difficult' business-cultures. Likewise, as also mentioned earlier, the Australian consultancy Anecdote is one of the best resources worldwide on 'business-storytelling' and other techniques to elicit and share the individual, context-dependent 'narrative knowledge' embedded in personal skills and experience. All strongly recommended, anyway.

Yet ultimately, the best way to build awareness in others is to *be* there with them. Tell a story about architecture: perhaps describe a scenario, the value and usefulness of a potential 'to-be'. Tell your *own* story; listen to theirs; work with them to find ways to help the stories align with each other. Often facts alone won't help all that much: what *does* help is the story, the *personal* nature and personal commitment implied in each story.

And the most powerful way to convey the meaning of a principle in practice is not just to 'tell' the story, but to *live* it by our own example. If architecture is about creating connections, integration of the whole *as* whole, then *we* need to be making those connections too, and learning from and with everyone as we go - the architects' equivalent of 'management by walking around'.

The enterprise *is* its people: those who "coordinate their functions and share information in support of a common mission" define what that shared 'mission' *is*. Those people are not 'assets': it is the *relationship* with each person that is the asset - and it's through those person-to-person connections around ideas of architecture that the awareness and the capability can coalesce.

The architecture is a shared body of knowledge to help the shared enterprise in decisions about its own structure and purpose. If some part of the purpose is changing, what changes in structures would we need, to support that change? What parts of those structures would change, and how, and why, and what else would be affected by those amendments and alterations? Given the structures we have, what purpose can we support, for each practical layer of 'purpose'? If we lose some part of the structure, what problems might that cause? If we change some part of the structure, what new options would that create for the enterprise as a whole? Architecture helps us to understand how structure and purpose interact, and hence helps us make the right choices for new directions.

We call ourselves 'enterprise architects', but that doesn't mean that we alone create the entire enterprise and its architecture - or any part of either of those, if we're to be honest about it. The reality is that the architecture is something we *co-create* with every other person in the enterprise, both within the organisation, and often also beyond the organisation's own borders, too. For that co-creation to happen, we must let go of command and control, share the load, and communicate, communicate, communicate.

The architecture *is* the dialogue; when we do allow the dialogue to become the architecture, the architecture in turn will become the enterprise. That's our real responsibility here: and as architects of the enterprise, it's up to us to make it so.

Resources

- Agile Manifesto: see agilemanifesto.org
- Agile Enterprise Architecture: see agileea.wikidot.com
- 'Hands-off' architecture: see chapter 'Methodology - hands-off architecture' in Tom Graves, *Bridging the Silos: enterprise architecture for IT-architects* (Tetradian, 2008)
- 'Open Space Technology': see www.openspaceworld.com

- Martin Leith, 'Leith's Guide to Large Group Interventions': see www.largescaleinterventions.com/documents/leiths_guide_to_lgis.pdf
- Theory on 'communities of practice': see www.ewenger.com/theory/
- Etienne Wenger, Richard McDermott and William M. Snyder, *Cultivating Communities of Practice: a guide to managing knowledge* (Harvard Business School Press, 2002)
- Narrative knowledge and business-storytelling: see www.anecdote.com.au
- Peter Senge et al., *The Dance of Change: the challenges of sustaining momentum in learning organizations* (Nicholas Brealey Publishing, 1999)
- Engagement in knowledge-sharing: see Chris Collison and Geoff Parcell, *Learning to Fly: practical lessons from one of the world's leading knowledge companies* (Capstone, 2001)

GLOSSARY

This summarises some of the terms and acronyms we've come across in the book.

ADM acronym for Architectural Design Method, the methodology used in *TOGAF* to guide development of *enterprise architecture*

ArchiMate a visual language used to model *enterprise architectures*, developed by Netherlands consortium Telematics

chaos domain in the *Cynefin* model, domain of inherent uncertainty and unpredictability; decisions are guided by *principles* and *values*; represented in the business context by unique market-of-one customisation and by non-repeatable maintenance issues; also useful when deliberately invoked in creativity, in *narrative* and dialogue, and in foresight techniques such as *scenario* construction

complex domain in the *Cynefin* model, domain of *emergent* properties and non-linear relationships between factors; decisions are derived from heuristics and guidelines; unlike *chaos*, which is inherently uncertain, may often create an illusion of predictability, especially where linear analysis is applied within a short-term, narrow set of assumptions

Cynefin model of organisational *complexity* developed by David Snowden of Cognitive Edge, which describes four distinct *paradigms* to interpret a given context: *known*, *knowable*, *complex* and *chaotic*

DyA acronym for Dynamic Architecture, an *enterprise-architecture* framework developed by Netherlands consultancy Sogeti

effective 'on purpose', producing the intended overall result with an *optimised* balance over the whole; requires broad generalist awareness of the whole, rather than the narrow focus required to create local efficiency, hence often contrasted with *efficient*

efficient 'doing more with less', creating the maximum result with minimum use or wastage of resources in a specific activity or context; improved incrementally through active learning and related techniques for feedback and reflection, although major improvements usually require a change in paradigm

emergence	context within which cause-effect patterns can be identified only retrospectively, and in which analytic techniques are usually unreliable and misleading
enterprise architecture	a systematic process to model and guide *integration* and *optimisation* of the information-technology of an enterprise or (at higher maturity-levels) the entire enterprise
FEAF	acronym for Federal Enterprise Architecture Framework, a framework and methodology developed for *enterprise architecture* by the US government
goal	a specific objective to be achieved by a specified point in time; emphasis on the physical or behavioural dimension of *purpose*, contrasted with *mission*, *role* and *vision*
knowable domain	in the *Cynefin* model, domain of 'the complicated', with identifiable cause-effect relationships; decisions are derived from contextual analysis
known domain	in the *Cynefin* model, domain of certainty and known cause-effect relationships; decisions are predefined by laws, rules and regulations
mission	a desired capability or state to be achieved, usually within a specified timeframe, and to be maintained indefinitely once achieved; emphasis on the relational and, to a lesser extent, the virtual dimensions of *purpose*, contrasted with *goal*, *role* and *vision*
narrative	personalised and often emotive expression or interpretation of knowledge, as history, anecdote or story
optimisation	process of *integration* in which *efficiency* in different areas is traded-off and balanced for maximum *effectiveness* over the whole, between different layers and sub-contexts such as departments, business processes and business units
principle	a conceptual commitment or model, the conceptual-dimension equivalent of *value*
purpose	an expression of individual and/or collective identity - the aspirational theme of "who we are and what we stand for"; incorporates distinct dimensions of *vision*, *role*, *mission* and *goal*
recursion	patterns of relationship or interaction repeat or are 'self-similar' at different scales; permits simplification of otherwise complex processes

role	a declared focus or *strategic* position within the 'world' described by a *vision*; emphasis on the conceptual and, to a lesser extent, the relational dimensions of *purpose*, contrasted with *goal*, *mission* and *vision*
scenario	an imagined future context, developed for the purpose of understanding both the present context and options for action in the future context
strategy	'big picture' view of an action-plan for an organisation to implement a *purpose*, usually emphasising its *vision*, *role* and *mission* components; contrasted with the *tactics* required to execute the plan
tactics	detailed *missions*, *goals* and other step-by-step activities to execute a *strategy*, or some segment of an overall strategy
TOGAF	acronym for The Open Group Architecture Framework, an IT-oriented framework and methodology for *enterprise architecture* developed collectively by members of the Open Group consortium
value	an emotional commitment
vision	description of a desired 'world', always far greater than any individual or organisation; described in the present tense, yet is never 'achieved'; emphasis on the aspirational dimension of *purpose*, contrasted with *goal*, *mission* and *role*
visioning	generic term for the process of identifying, developing and documenting *vision* and *values*, leading towards *strategy* and *tactics*
Zachman framework	a systematic structure for categorisation of models within an IT-oriented *enterprise architecture*, developed by John Zachman

CPSIA information can be obtained at www.ICGtesting.com
Printed in the USA
BVOW04s0305240714

360104BV00016B/53/P